Anonymus

Returns of local taxation in Ireland

1895

Anonymus

Returns of local taxation in Ireland
1895

ISBN/EAN: 9783742801272

Manufactured in Europe, USA, Canada, Australia, Japa

Cover: Foto ©ninafisch / pixelio.de

Manufactured and distributed by brebook publishing software
(www.brebook.com)

Anonymus

Returns of local taxation in Ireland

LOCAL TAXATION (IRELAND) RETURNS.

RETURNS

OF

LOCAL TAXATION IN IRELAND

FOR THE

YEAR 1895,

COLLECTED AND COMPILED, BY DESIRE OF

HIS EXCELLENCY THE LORD LIEUTENANT,

BY

THE LOCAL GOVERNMENT BOARD FOR IRELAND.

Presented to Parliament by Command of Her Majesty.

DUBLIN:
PRINTED FOR HER MAJESTY'S STATIONERY OFFICE,
BY ALEXANDER THOM & CO. (LIMITED).

And to be purchased, either directly or through any Bookseller, from
Hodges, Figgis, and Co. (Limited), 104, Grafton-street, Dublin; or
Eyre and Spottiswoode, East Harding-street, Fleet-street, E.C.; or
John Menzies and Co., 12, Hanover-street, Edinburgh, and 90, West Nile-street, Glasgow.

1896.

TABLE OF CONTENTS.

INTRODUCTORY AND EXPLANATORY OBSERVATIONS.

APPENDICES.

Returns of local taxation classified according to the objects to which taxation is applied.

INTRODUCTORY AND EXPLANATORY OBSERVATIONS.

1. TOTAL AMOUNT OF LOCAL TAXATION IN IRELAND.

THE local taxation of Ireland, making the deductions ascertained to be necessary on account of duplicate entries, and supplying the absence of a certain return* by the latest information available, may be set down for the year 1895 at £3,842,005, being an increase of £92,583, or 2·4 per cent., on the amount in the previous year.

The various local rates and taxes are arranged in the following table to show the distribution of this amount under the heads of Rates on real property, Tolls, fees, stamps and dues, and other sources of receipt, apart from loans, and grants from the Imperial taxes; as also the increase or decrease in the amount of each branch of taxation compared with the year 1894.

Local Taxes.	Rates on real property.	Tolls, fees, stamps, and dues.	Other receipts.	Total.	Increase as compared with 1894.	Decrease as compared with 1894.
1	2	3	4	5	6	7
	£	£	£	£	£	£
Grand Jury Cess,	1,263,839	—	14,349	1,278,188	50,001	—
Poor rate,	1,025,619	—	45,359	1,070,978	87,778	—
Town taxes,	441,788	47,176	183,674	672,638	84	—
Belfast Water rate,	27,918	—	22,809	50,727	5,317	—
Rutland-square tax (Dublin),	281	—	—	281	6	—
Dublin Metropolitan Police taxes,	34,962	10,363	4,774	50,004	—	872
Dublin Port and Docks Board taxes,	8,742	—	421	9,163	4,158	—
Court Leet Presentments,	—	—	—	—	—	—
Burial board receipts,	—	83	124	207	61	—
Fees of Clerks of the Peace,	—	3,418	—	3,418	—	769
Fees of Clerks of the Crown,	—	310	—	310	—	91
Petty Sessions stamps and Crown fees,	—	49,894	5,881	55,777	—	407
Dogs licence duty,	—	41,979	389	42,368	516	—
Harbour taxation,	—	312,196	62,744	374,940	7,808	—
Inland navigation taxation,	—	3,740	2,619	6,359	—	118
Light dues, and fees under Merchant Shipping Act,	—	19,637	—	19,637	—	464
Total, 1895	3,005,456	469,844	369,706	3,842,005	Net increase.	—
Total, 1894	2,941,540	480,557	317,875	3,749,422	92,583	
Increase,	63,916	—	52,831	92,583		
Decrease,	—	8,713	—	—		

* See notes at foot of Table II. on pages 24 and 25.

The amount of the local taxation of Ireland in the year 1895 was therefore produced as follows:

	£		Per cent.
Rates on real property, . .	3,035,483	or	78·83 of the total amount.
Tolls, Fees, Stamps, and Dues, .	456,816	"	11·87 " "
Other receipts, . . .	349,706	"	9·1 " "
Total, . .	£3,842,005		100

Of the other receipts included in the taxation of 1895, amounting to £349,706, a considerable portion has been derived from certain sources which are referred to under the following heads, (a) and (b).

Gas and Water Undertakings (a.)

Gas.

The revenues arising from the gas undertakings which are in the hands of certain town authorities are dealt with in the returns of local taxation in the following manner. The gas accounts are kept apart from the other accounts of those authorities, and in any case in which a profit has accrued on a year's transactions after providing for the lighting of the town, this profit, unless otherwise applied by the town authority, is brought forward in aid of the local rate, and is included in the abstract of the town accounts given in the appendices under the head of other receipts. The total amount of such profits included in column 4 of the foregoing table for the year 1895 is £11,182.

Water.

The receipts connected with water undertakings in the hands of local taxing authorities are two-fold,—those produced by poundage rates assessed on valuation, and those arising from sales of water, water rents, &c. The latter are included under the head of other receipts in the returns of local taxation, and in 1895 they amounted to £66,979.

As regards the sums produced by public and domestic water rates assessed on valuation, it is to be noted that these are included in the amount given under the head of rates on real property, but the accounts of these rates are not always kept separately, and therefore it is not possible to determine with accuracy the amount produced by each of them in the course of a year. It is estimated, however, that of the total amount of water rates appearing in the accounts of 1895, viz., £115,970, a sum of £57,868 was for water supplied for private purposes.*

Bounty in lieu of rates of Government property (b.)

The contributions paid by the Treasury to local authorities in respect of rates on Government property are also included in other receipts, and the amount thereof in the accounts of 1895 was £33,833. The distribution of this sum among the local taxing bodies was as follows:—

	£
Town Authorities, ...	20,415
Boards of Guardians, ...	6,706
Grand Juries, ...	5,300
Dublin Port and Docks Board, . . .	413
Total, .	£33,833

The bounty in lieu of rates on Government property has been paid to local taxing bodies in Ireland in each year since 1874.

* The water rates in the accounts of 1894 amounted to £117,397, of which, approximately, a sum of £72,770 was for water supplied for private purposes.

Grants from the Imperial Taxes in aid of Local Rates.

In addition to the contributions paid by the Treasury to local authorities as rates on Government property, the following grants from the Imperial taxes were made to the three authorities first named hereafter in respect of the year ended the 31st of March, 1895. In the remaining cases the sums named appear in the accounts of the year 1895. The grants marked (*a*) and (*c*) have been paid each year since 1867, those marked (*b*) and (*d*) in each year since 1875, the amounts necessarily varying in each year. As already observed the grants from the Imperial taxes in aid of local rates are not included in the amount of the year's taxation given on page 5.

			£
Boards of Guardians,	(*a*)	One half the salaries of medical officers of Dispensary Districts and of Workhouses, and one half the cost of medicines,	74,[illegible]
	(*b*)	A proportionate amount of salaries paid in Rural Sanitary Districts under the Public Health Acts, as fixed by scale,	11,869
	(*c*)	The salaries of teachers in Workhouses,	9,381
		Grant under the Probate Duties (Scotland and Ireland) Act, 1888,	92,867
		Grant under the Local Taxation (Customs and Excise) Act, 1890, paid to 32 Unions, which are contributory Unions as defined by the National School Teachers Act, 1875,	16,996
Grand Juries,		Grant under the Probate Duties (Scotland and Ireland) Act, 1888,	73,143
Urban Sanitary Authorities (*d*)		A proportionate amount of the salaries paid in Urban Sanitary Districts under the Public Health Acts, as fixed by scale,	4,730
		Grant under the Probate Duties (Scotland and Ireland) Act, 1888, to the Governing Bodies of thirty-two towns,* who maintain their own roads and streets, to the exclusion of Grand Juries,	17,423
Harbours under Commissioners of Public Works,			18,116
Navigations under Commissioners of Public Works,			403
Clerks of the Peace,			1,028
Clerks of the Crown,			1,025
		Total,	333,344

* These towns, and the amount of Probate Duty Grant received by each of them, will be found in the table on page 59.

TABLE SHOWING THE AMOUNT RAISED BY LOCAL TAXATION IN EACH OF THE LAST TWENTY-ONE YEARS.

Year.	Local taxation of Ireland.	Increase as compared to preceding year.	Decrease as compared to preceding year.	Increase per cent.	Decrease per cent.
	£	£	£		
1875, . . .	3,192,945	48,617	—	1·6	—
1876, . . .	3,242,093	49,148	—	1·6	—
1877, . . .	3,168,113	—	73,980	—	2·4
1878, . . .	3,253,422	85,309	—	2·7	—
1879, . . .	3,368,113	116,891	—	3·6	—
1880, . . .	3,292,541	—	75,572	—	2·2
1881, . . .	3,391,430	98,889	—	3	—
1882, . . .	3,534,579	143,149	—	4·2	—
1883, . . .	3,778,815	243,536	—	6·9	—
1884, . . .	3,789,040	10,448	—	·3	—
1885, . . .	3,582,130	—	207,820	—	5·4
1886, . . .	3,492,672	—	189,448	—	2·5
1887, . . .	3,540,103	47,431	—	1·4	—
1888, . . .	3,575,472	35,369	—	1	—
1889, . . .	3,663,207	87,736	—	2·5	—
1890, . . .	3,560,093	—	104,114	—	2·8
1891, . . .	3,503,519	—	56,574	—	1·6
1892, . . .	3,589,239	85,720	—	2·4	—
1893, . . .	3,704,434	114,195	—	3·2	—
1894, . . .	3,749,429	44,995	—	1·2	—
1895, . . .	3,843,036	93,563	—	2·4	—

CLASSIFICATION OF LOCAL TAXATION.

The various branches of local taxation in Ireland are classified hereinafter in the following manner, to correspond with the arrangement in column 1 of the table on page 5, and such observations as appeared to be necessary in regard to the nature and extent of taxation, the rating powers conferred on local authorities, the areas of taxation enlarged in certain cases by the legislation of 1896, the poundage rates made for the expenditure of 1895, &c., are prefixed in each case :—

I. County taxation.
II. Union ,,
III. Municipal ,,
IV. Taxation in districts chiefly municipal, but not levied by municipal bodies.
V. Receipts of Burial Boards.
VI. Taxation arising from Fees, Stamps, Fines, Dogs' Licence Duty, &c.
VII. Taxation produced by Tolls, Dues, &c.
VIII. Receipts on account of the Mercantile Marine Fund.

I.—COUNTY TAXATION.

Grand Jury Cess.

One of the oldest of the local taxes in Ireland and that which produces the largest amount of taxation is the poundage rate on real property called Grand Jury Cess, or County Cess. The area of incidence in the case of this rate is, in counties other than counties of cities and of towns, the Barony or half Barony, and in counties of cities and of towns the County; and, as there are 326* baronies and half baronies, and 8 counties of cities and of towns, there are 334 separate areas of taxation for the purposes of county administration.

The cess is levied on the occupier according to the area of taxation in which his holding is situated, but in the case of any tenancy created since the 1st of August 1870 of which the valuation does not exceed £4, it is provided by the Landlord and Tenant Act of that year that the cess shall be payable by the immediate lessor,—a similar provision in regard to poor rate having been enacted in 1843. Section 65 of this Statute, moreover, with respect to lettings made at any date subsequent to its enactment, applied to Grand Jury Cess the principle of dividing the rate equally between the rated occupier and owner by enabling the former to deduct one-half the cess paid by him from his rent; an arrangement which has been in operation in regard to the poor rate since the introduction of the Poor Laws in 1838.

Presentments.

The purposes to which Grand Jury Cess is applied, and the gross amount of the presentments passed in 1895 for each branch of county expenditure are shown in the following summary of the table on pages 22 and 23.

		£	Per centage of total.
Roads, footways, bridges, &c.,		766,915	51·29
Maintenance of lunatic asylums,		165,845	11·1
Miscellaneous,		231,867	15·47
Salaries of County officers,		96,319	6·47
Prison expenses,		17,387	1·16
In discharge of debt:—			
To Government,	£80,400		
To others than Government,	7,250		
		87,650	5·85
Infirmaries, hospitals, &c.,		83,195	5·57
Extra police,		21,811	1·46
Valuation,		8,650	·58
Erection and repairs of Court and Sessions' houses,		10,444	·7
Police for weights and measures,		4,480	·30
Total,		£1,495,851	100

The re-presentments and credits available towards this total amounted to £171,939, and the deduction of this sum left a net amount of £1,323,912 to be levied in 1895, an increase of £19,609 on the amount of the levy in 1894.

The sums presented for the construction, maintenance, and repairs of roads, footways, bridges, &c., in the year 1895 amounted to £766,915, being £959 less than in the preceding year, and forming, as will be seen by the foregoing summary, 51·29 per cent. of the total presentments, that is, practically about one-half, as is usually the case. The next largest sum is that under the heading miscellaneous, amounting to £231,867, and in this is included the cost of registration of Parliamentary Voters, Jurors' expenses, compensation for malicious injuries, cost of collection of the cess, printing, &c. The presentments for lunatic asylums amounted to £165,845, being £17,165 in excess of the amount in the preceding year, and for prison expenses to £17,387. The

* The actual number is 327, but two baronies in the county of Carlow are united for purposes of taxation.

cost of the maintenance of prisons in Ireland was formerly borne by the Grand Jury Cess, but under the General Prisons Act, 1877, it is now defrayed from moneys voted by Parliament, and the foregoing sum provides chiefly for the annuities paid to former prison officers, £12,830 being required for this purpose, as against £18,050 in 1894. The presentments for extra police amounted to £21,811, being £4,870 less than in the preceding year.* The charge for valuation in each county is fixed by the Act 37 and 38 Vic., cap. 70, at the respective amounts given in column 12 of the table on page 23, making a total of £8,000. The presentments under the remaining heads do not call for any special observations, and exhibit no very marked differences from the amounts under the corresponding heads in the returns of the preceding year.

Poundage of Grand Jury Cess.

The average poundage of the Grand Jury Cess levied in 1895 in each county, and county of a city, and county of a town is given in column 20 of the table on page 23, and it will be seen thereby that the highest average was reached in Kerry, viz., 4s. 6¾d., and the lowest in Meath, viz., 1s. 0¼d., while the average for the whole of Ireland was 2s. 1d. By provinces, the average cess ranged in Ulster from 1s. 8d. in Fermanagh to 3s. 5¼d. in Donegal, in Munster from 1s. 8¾d. in Limerick county of the city to 4s. 6¾d. in Kerry, in Leinster from 1s. 0¼d. in Meath to 3s. 7d. in Kilkenny county of the city, and in Connaught from 1s. 6¾d. in Roscommon to 2s. 9¾d. in Leitrim.

The average poundages of the cess levied in the preceding year are given in column 21 of the same table for the purpose of comparison.

Receipts of County Authorities.

The receipts of each county authority during 1895, with the exception of those of the counties of the cities of Cork, Dublin and Limerick, will be found in a table on page 24 which has been compiled from the abstracts of county accounts furnished by the Auditors of the Local Government Board, and they are summarised as follows:—

Receipts.	£	Per centage of total.
Amount of Grand Jury cess collected,	1,263,839	87·63
From the Imperial taxes,	[illegible]	[illegible]
From local rates or taxes,	[illegible]	·91
From loans,	6,337	·44
From other sources (including £14,558 received from the Dogs License Duty),	[illegible]	[illegible]
Total,	£1,438,048	100

The fiscal powers of the Grand Juries of the three counties of cities named above have been transferred by special legislation to the respective Municipal Councils,† and the receipts on account of the rates levied in lieu of Grand Jury Cess in these counties of cities are included in municipal taxation in table IV., on page 36.

To these three counties of cities Waterford must now be added—the fiscal powers of the Grand Jury having been transferred to the Municipal Council from the 1st of September, 1898, by an Act of last Session, 59 and 60 Vic., cap. cxxv. As bearing on the question of taxation it may be mentioned here that under this Statute the area of the city of Waterford has been enlarged, thereby increasing its valuation for rating purposes, that jurisdiction with respect to roads, bridges, &c., in the added area has been transferred to the Corporation, that additional rating powers have been conferred on that Body, and that by Section 57 the city will participate in the grant provided by the Probate Duties (Scotland and Ireland) Act, 1888, in every year after the 31st of December, 1897.

* The cost of police in Ireland is referred to on page 17.

† The Statutes, respectively, are 15 & 16 Vic., cap. cxiii., 12 & 13 Vic., cap. 97, and 16 & 17 Vic., cap. cxxix.

The Town Council of another Borough named in the Municipal Corporations (Ireland) Act, 1840, viz., Drogheda, obtained special legislation with respect to their municipality during last Session (59 and 60 Vic., cap. ccxx), but in this case, while the area of the town has been extended, the Grand Jury of the county of the town of Drogheda retain their powers within the old area, and will become the Road Authority in the added area from and after the Summer assizes of 1897.

Valuation of Counties.

The valuation of each county, and county of a city, and county of a town in Ireland in 1896, and in each of the four preceding years will be found on page 60, from which it may be seen that the total valuation of the country has increased from £14,081,062 in 1892 to £14,396,540 in 1896. The increase, amounting to £315,478, has taken place chiefly in the counties of Antrim and Down, and is mainly attributable to the growth of the city of Belfast, the valuation of which has increased from £716,502 in the former year to £887,281 in the latter, an increase of £170,779. The valuation of Belfast as given herein does not include that of the area added to the city by an Act of last Session, 59 and 60 Vic., cap. ccxlvi.

II.—UNION TAXATION.

Poor Rate.

The taxation produced by the Poor Rate levied by Boards of Guardians in Poor Law Unions ranks next in amount to that produced by the Grand Jury Cess. This rate is also a poundage on valuation, and, with the following exceptions, is assessed on occupiers according to the Electoral Division in which the occupied property is situate, there being a distinct rate for each Electoral Division.

The rating of the immediate lessor instead of the occupier is provided for by section 1 of the Act 6 and 7 Vic., cap. 92, in cases where the valuation of the occupied property does not exceed £4, subject to certain exceptions as set forth in the section. Section 4 of this Act provides that immediate lessors shall be rated for houses let in separate apartments or lodgings, and under section 10 of the Act 12 and 13 Vict., cap. 104, persons receiving rent in respect of hereditaments exempt from rating are liable to be rated in respect of such rent to the extent of one-half the poundage rate on the Electoral Division in which the hereditaments are situated. Section 63 of the Act 12 and 13 Vict., cap. 91, provides that, in the City of Dublin, the owner of property of which the valuation does not exceed £8, or which is let to weekly or monthly tenants, or in separate apartments, shall be rated instead of the occupier.

Number of Unions, Electoral Divisions, &c.

There are at the present time 159 Poor Law Unions, embracing 3,441 Electoral Divisions, and the average number of divisions in each Union is therefore nearly 22. The greatest number comprised in a Union is 48 in the case of Mullingar, and the smallest 7, in the cases of Castlecomer and Castletown Unions.

In 1895 the valuation of the Unions on which the Poor Rate was assessed varied from £976,025 in Belfast to £10,818 in Belmullet, the average valuation being £89,676.

Rural Sanitary Authorities.

Under Section 6 of the Public Health (Ireland) Act, 1878, all Boards of Guardians are Rural Sanitary Authorities over such portions of their respective Unions as are not contained in Urban Sanitary Districts, and they levy the necessary rates for carrying out the provisions of the Acts relating to public health in the areas within their jurisdiction as part of the poor rate. The expenses of a rural Sanitary Authority are by section 232 divided into general expenses and special expenses, the former being payable out of the poor rate of the Electoral Divisions or parts thereof included in the entire sanitary district, according to valuation, the latter being chargeable to some contributory place or contributory places as defined by the section.

Private improvement expenses which a Rural Sanitary Authority may have incurred, or for which they may be liable, can now be provided for by a private improvement rate which the Rural Authority are empowered to make and levy by Section 4 of the Public Health (Ireland) Act, 1896.

Poundage of Poor Rate.

The poor rate levied in the Electoral Divisions for the expenditure of the year ended in 1895 ranged as follows:—

		s. d.		s. d.	
Ulster,	From	0 8	to	6 10	this maximum being reached in the case of one Division.
Munster,	"	0 8	"	5 0	" " " three Divisions.
Leinster,	"	0 2	"	4 0	" " " one Division.
Connaught,	"	0 6	"	5 11	" " " three Divisions.

The average poundage of the total amount assessed in Ulster was 0s. 10½d., in Munster 2s. 0¼d., in Leinster 1s. 6d., in Connaught 1s. 7½d.; and the average poor rate for all Ireland was 1s. 6½d.

Receipts and Expenditure of Boards of Guardians.

The particulars of the collection and expenditure of the poor rate are fully set forth in the Annual Reports of the Local Government Board, and it is not considered necessary to insert here any fuller statement on the subject than the following brief summary, which shows the aggregate receipts of Boards of Guardians, the several purposes to which the poor rate is applied, and the amount expended under each head of outlay in the year ended in 1895.

Receipts and expenditure during the year ended the 29th of September, 1895, exclusive of receipts and payments under the Seed Supply Acts.

Receipts.	£
Poor Rate lodged,	[illegible]
Parliamentary Grants,	[illegible]
Other receipts,	[illegible]
Loans,	[illegible]
Total,	£1,454,170

Expenditure.	£
In-Maintenance,	[illegible]
Out-Relief,	[illegible]
Maintenance of Blind and Deaf and Dumb in Institutions, and cost of relief in certain hospitals,	[illegible]
Salaries and rations of officers,	[illegible]
Emigration expenses,	[illegible]
All other Poor Relief expenses,	[illegible]
Poor Relief expenditure,	[illegible]
Medical Charities, Vaccination, and Dispensary Houses Acts,	[illegible]
Lunatic Asylums Act (Fees for examination of Lunatics),	[illegible]
Acts for Registration of Births, Deaths, and Marriages,	[illegible]
Public Health Acts,	[illegible]
Burial Grounds,	[illegible]
Superannuation Acts,	[illegible]
Contagious Diseases (Animals) Acts,	[illegible]
Payments under National School Teachers Act,	[illegible]
Payments under the Technical Instruction Act,	[illegible]
Labourers Acts,	[illegible]
Parliamentary Franchise Acts,	[illegible]
Jurors Act,	[illegible]
Explosives Act,	[illegible]
Repayment of loans,	[illegible]
Total expenditure,	[illegible]

The expenditure under the Labourers Acts, Public Health Acts, and other Acts given in the foregoing summary was largely defrayed from loans, and the deduction of the amounts so defrayed gives the net expenditure for poor relief £861,706, and the net total expenditure £1,325,300.

The net expenditure in each Province, and the poundages thereof on valuation are shown in the following table:—

—	Poor Relief Expenditure.	Poundage on Valuation.	Total Expenditure.	Poundage on Valuation.	Poundage or Rate levied for other purposes than the relief of the poor.
	£	s. d.	£	s. d.	s. d.
Ulster, ...	174,877	0 9	[illegible]	1 [illegible]	0 6
Munster, . . .	[illegible]	1 6	441,779	2 6½	0 10½
Leinster, . .	304,216	1 3½	451,194	1 10½	0 7½
Connaught, . . .	83,976	1 4½	141,[illegible]	2 0½	0 8½
Total, Ireland, . .	861,706	1 3½	1,325,300	1 10½	0 7½

III.—MUNICIPAL TAXATION.

Town Rates.

There are at the present time 119 towns in Ireland under municipal government, and, with the exception of Bantry hereafter referred to, they are classified in four tables given in the Appendix, viz., tables IV., V., VI., and VII., in accordance with the Statutes under which the governing bodies were constituted at the time the rates dealt with in these tables were assessed. These Statutes are:—

3 & 4 Vic., cap. 108, under which there are 11 towns governed by Town Councils,

17 & 18 Vic., cap. 103, " " 89 " " " " Commissioners,

9 Geo. IV., cap. 82, " " 6 " " " " "

And, Special Acts, " " 13 " and townships governed by Commissioners.

There is one other town, Carrickfergus, referred to on page 15, which is governed by Municipal Commissioners under Section 16 of the first named Act, and section 25 of 6 and 7 Vic., cap. 93, and it is placed in table VII. for purposes of convenience.

The number of towns constituted under the second Statute named above, the Towns Improvement (Ireland) Act, 1854, was increased by two during the year 1896, viz., Bantry, in which the Act was adopted in accordance with the usual procedure in the month of July, and Armagh, to which it was applied from the 1st of November by the Statute 59 & 60 Vic., cap. ccxxxv. Up to the date mentioned Armagh had been constituted under 9 George IV., cap. 82.

The rate levied in towns is a poundage on valuation, and the following are the rating powers conferred on municipal authorities by the Legislature in the three general Acts specified above.

Section 138 of the Act 3 & 4 Vic., cap. 108 the Municipal Corporations (Ireland) Act, 1840, authorises the Council of a borough to levy a rate on the owners, occupiers or tenants of hereditaments situated therein, subject to the proviso contained in the section with regard to hereditaments under the value of £3, viz., that only those persons who are rated under the Poor Relief Acts in respect of such hereditaments within the borough shall be liable to pay this rate. Section 10 of the amending Act, 3 & 4 Vic., cap. 109, directs that the maximum borough rate in any borough shall be 1s. in the £, and except in certain cases it limits this rate in boroughs in which the Act 9 Geo. IV., cap. 82, is in force to 6d. The provisions of the Act 17 and 18 Vic., cap. 103, are wholly or partly in operation in six of the towns constituted under the Act 3 and 4 Vic., cap. 108, the remaining five being debarred by Section 100 from adopting it. The municipal Council in each of these five cases, however, possess additional powers of taxation under local Acts.

In towns under 17 & 18 Vic., cap. 103, the Towns Improvement (Ireland) Act, 1854, the rate is made on the occupier where the valuation of the occupied property exceeds £4, and, except in certain cases, on the immediate lessor, when it does not exceed that amount. The rate is limited to 1s., save in those towns where the Commissioners supply water to the ratepayers under the provisions of the Act, and in such cases it is limited to 1s. 6d. Section 62 provides that certain lands, as therein described, shall be rated on one-fourth only of their valuation.

In towns under the Act 9 George IV., cap. 82, the Lighting of Towns (Ireland) Act, 1828, the rate is levied on the owners, occupiers, or tenants of property within the town; and for the purposes of the rate the property is classified as follows:—

Tenements valued at £5 and under £10, in which cases the poundage cannot exceed 6d. in the £, those valued at £10 and under £20, in which it cannot exceed 9d., and those valued at £20 and upwards, in which it cannot exceed 1s. It is also provided that the rate on the class of tenements first mentioned shall be equal to two-thirds of that on those in the second class, and one-half of that on those in the third class, and that the rate on the second class shall be equal to three-fourths of that on those in the third class. Premises under £5 valuation are exempt from rating. There are only six towns at the present time constituted under this Statute, as will be seen above, and, by section 19 of the Towns Improvement Act, its provisions cannot be adopted in any town since the 10th of August, 1854.

As regards the towns constituted under special Acts, the provisions of the Towns Improvement Act, either in whole or part, have been incorporated with the local Act in almost every case.

Urban Sanitary Districts.

A further classification of the towns as Urban Sanitary Districts, of which there are now 73, Portrush being constituted such by an Act of last Session, 59 & 60 Vic., cap. lxxvii., and those which are not Urban Sanitary Districts of which the number is 46, will be found on pages 58 and 59. The governing bodies of the former are Urban Sanitary Authorities, and under section 238 of the Public Health Act, 1878, the expenses payable by them in the execution of the Acts relating to public health are defrayed, in the case of the Council of a borough out of the borough fund or borough rate, and in other cases, out of any rate leviable by the governing body throughout their whole district. Urban Sanitary Authorities are also empowered by Section 229 to make and levy a private improvement rate for the purpose of discharging any expenses which they may have incurred, or to which they may become liable, as private improvement expenses.

Rates under the Housing of the Working Classes Act.

The Housing of the Working Classes Act, 53 and 54 Vic., cap. 70, confers certain powers on local authorities in relation to the clearing of unhealthy areas or unhealthy dwellings, and the erection of lodging-houses for the working classes, and the necessary expenses are defrayed out of the local rate as defined in the 1st Schedule to the Act. Section 24 removes for the purposes of Part I, which deals with unhealthy areas, any limit imposed on or in respect of local rates. Section 42 similarly removes for the purpose of Part 2, which deals with unhealthy dwelling-houses, any existing limit on local rates, and Section 65 provides that expenses incurred for the purpose of Part 3, which deals with the erection of working classes lodging-houses, shall be defrayed as part of the expenses under the Public Health Act. As regards Town Commissioners who are not Sanitary Authorities, it is provided by Section 99 that their local rate may, with the approval of the Treasury, be increased for the purpose of carrying out Part 3 of the Act.

Poundage of town rates.

The tables on pages 58 and 59, give the town rates levied for the expenditure of the year 1895, and it will be seen thereby that in urban sanitary districts the poundages varied from 6d. in Cootehill and Kilrush to 6s. 5½d. in the city of Cork. This latter is an aggregate poundage, and includes, amongst others, the "General Purposes Rate" levied in lieu of Grand Jury Cess, which appears from column 20 of table 1 of the Appendices to have been 1s. 6d. Similarly in the cases of Dublin and Limerick cities, the respective rates of 4s. 10d. and 5s. 8d. include the rates in lieu of Grand Jury Cess given in the same table—viz., 1s. 4½d. and 1s. 3½d. respectively. The rate of 3s. 4d. in the case of Belfast includes a police rate of 1s. 4d. in the £ on valuations above £20, and 8d. in the £ on valuations of £20 and under, which is levied under the Act 8 and 9 Vic., cap. 142. In the towns which are not urban sanitary districts the rates varied from 4d. in Cookstown to 2s. in Arklow. This latter, however, includes 1s. which the Commissioners are required by section 7 of the Act 45 Vic., cap. 13, to levy as an additional rate to that under the Towns Improvement Act for the repayment of a certain portion of the expenditure incurred in connection with Arklow Harbour.

Towns wholly or partly exempt from rates.

It will be seen by the tables referred to in the preceding paragraph that no rates were assessed in the following towns:—Carrickfergus, Cashel, Drogheda, Kells, Clonakilty, Tuam, Belturbet, Callan, Fethard, and Kilkenny. The municipal revenue is derived in each of the first four cases from real property, in the next two from tolls levied at markets and fairs, and in the last four partly from tolls and partly from property. The Corporation of Waterford and the Commissioners of Wicklow are possessed of sufficient income to render the levying of rates for ordinary municipal purposes unnecessary, those given in the table being in each case levied in connection with a supply of water provided by the town Authority. Many towns have a considerable revenue arising from property, market tolls, and other permanent sources of income, and the sums received under these heads, in addition to the produce of the rates assessed are, in every case, set forth in the town returns in the Appendices. In the case of Trim, it may be mentioned, that the property vested in the Commissioners procured the town an exemption from rates until 1894.

The Municipal Commissioners of the town of Carrickfergus, already referred to, have no power to levy rates for ordinary purposes, but by an Act of the Session of 1895, 58 & 59 Vic., cap. lxxi., the area over which they exercise jurisdiction, viz., the County of the Town of Carrickfergus, has been divided into an Urban Sanitary District and a Rural Sanitary District, and the Commissioners have been constituted the Sanitary Authority of each District, and have been invested with power to make a separate rate for each District to enable them to defray the expenditure incurred in carrying the Public Health Acts into execution.

Valuation, Population, and Area of towns.

The valuation, population, and area of each town, together with the Act or Acts under which each is constituted, will be found on pages 58 and 59.

Roads and streets maintained by town authorities.

The towns in which the roads and streets are maintained by the governing bodies to the exclusion of Grand Juries, together with such county charges as are contributed to from the town rates in these cases, are shown on pages 61 to 64.

Receipts and Expenditure of Town Authorities.

The receipts of the various municipal authorities are grouped together in Part I. of the following table to facilitate comparison of the amounts collected by the different classes of town authorities, and they are divided into—(1) rates on real property; (2) tolls and market charges, dues, and fees; (3) from rents and other sources; (4) from borrowed money and the issue of stock; (5) from the Imperial taxes; and (6) from Grand Jury cess, or other local tax.

The various purposes to which town rates are applied are shown in Part II., below.

Part I.—Receipts.

Receipts.	Towns under Town Councils.	Towns having Commissioners under Act of 1854.	Towns under Lighting and Cleansing Commissioners.	Towns having Commissioners under special Acts.	Total Receipts.	Per cent.
	£	£	£	£	£	
1. Rates on real property,	476,807	*58,188	3,370	104,318	642,788	49·53
2. Tolls, and Market charges, Dues, and Fees,	24,425	7,562	51	9,144	47,178	3·63
3. Rents, and other sources,	179,606	21,859	2,893	13,060	216,924	16·71
4. From borrowed money and from the issue of stock,	250,524	38,799	5,300	48,413	342,999	26·43
5. From the Imperial taxes,	25,183	1,663	39	3,941	30,833	2·38
6. From Grand Jury cess, or other local tax,	13,748	2,794	80	443	17,065	1·29
Total,	951,031	131,393	12,143	183,341	1,297,797	100

It appears from this table, that of the total receipts of town authorities in Ireland—£1,297,797—£642,788, or 49·53 per cent., was from rates on real property; £342,999, or 26·43 per cent., was from money borrowed on the security of the rates and realised by the issue of stock; £216,924, or 16·71 per cent., was from rents and other sources; £47,178, or 3·63 per cent., was from tolls and market charges, dues, and fees; £30,833, or 2·38 per cent., was from the Imperial taxes; and £17,065, or 1·29 per cent., was from Grand Jury cess, or other local tax.

Part II.—Expenditure.

Expenditure.	Towns under Town Councils.	Towns having Commissioners under Act of 1854.	Towns under Lighting and Cleansing Commissioners.	Towns having Commissioners under special Acts.	Total expenditure.	Per cent.
	£	£	£	£	£	
Payments in respect of borrowed money, and expenditure unclassed,	437,651	36,716	4,113	105,597	584,178	45·16
Water supply,	46,257	35,185	6,154	18,543	106,140	7·92
Paving and repairs of streets,	136,479	10,019	430	90,738	163,857	12·83
County charges paid out of Grand Jury cess by Town Councils, and payments in aid of Grand Jury cess,	73,564	3,070	—	10,153	87,807	6·43
Building, demolition of walls, &c.,	60,029	6,330	—	11,799	77,730	6·06
Lighting, including lamps, pipes, &c.,	43,088	9,828	1,478	9,881	64,738	4·63
Making sewers or drains, and for other sanitary purposes,	91,684	4,749	847	17,833	118,970	8·91
Cleansing and watering streets,	84,083	5,584	446	4,645	93,108	7·1
Watching,	15,010	360	239	107	15,716	1·17
Total,	936,770	154,867	11,100	196,340	1,340,077	100

* A sum of £1,339 has been excluded here for the reasons set forth in the second note on page 30.

IV.—TAXATION IN DISTRICTS CHIEFLY MUNICIPAL, BUT NOT LEVIED BY MUNICIPAL BODIES.

(a.) Belfast Water Rate.

The Belfast City and District Water Commissioners are empowered to levy the following rates in the Borough of Belfast and the suburban districts,—a domestic water rate not exceeding 1s. 6d. in the pound, and a public water rate equal to one-fourth part of the domestic rate, subject to a proviso that the latter in certain cases shall be only 2d. in the pound. The domestic water rate assessed for the year 1895 was 1s. in the pound.

The receipts and expenditure of the Commissioners, which are included in table VII. of the Appendices for purposes of convenience, are summarized as follows:—

Receipts.	£	Expenditure.	£
Rates,	67,918	Water supply,	31,818
Money borrowed,	110,983	Payments on account of borrowed money,	102,658
From local taxes,	687	Other expenses,	1,300
Other receipts,	16,879		
Total,	£196,?96	Total,	£135,876

(b.) Rutland-square Tax (Dublin).

Under the Act 25 George 3, cap. 48 (Ireland), sections 20 and 21, the Governors of the Rotunda Hospital levy a tax on the occupiers of the houses on the east, north, and west sides of Rutland-square for the purpose of lighting those sides of the square, and for keeping the railings of the enclosure in repair, the balance to be applied towards the maintenance of the hospital. This tax is not a poundage on valuation like all other taxes on real property dealt with in these returns, but is a charge on each house in the square of 1s. 3d. per foot of the frontage thereof, together with a fixed annual payment by the residents for each light or lamp in front of their houses. These are calculated to produce annually a sum of £307 19s. 1d., of which there was received in 1895 £280 17s. 9d., £120 17s. 0d. being applied to purposes of lighting and £160 0s. 9d. in aid of the hospital. The receipts and expenditure in this case are also included in table VII.

(c.) Taxation in aid of the cost of the Dublin Metropolitan Police.

Under Section 4 of the Act 1 and 2 Vic., cap. 25, a rate of 8d. in the pound on valuation is assessed within the police district of Dublin Metropolis, as defined in the Act, in aid of the cost of the Dublin Metropolitan Police, and the amount produced thereby, together with the sums received from pawnbrokers' licences, publicans' certificates, &c., which were paid over to the Treasury for the year ended the 31st of March, 1896, are given in table VIII., of which the following is a summary:—

	£	£
Rates on houses and land,	26,323	
Carriage duty,	3,575	
		29,898
Taxes peculiar to Dublin:—		
Pawnbrokers' licences,	4,608	
Publicans' and grocers' certificates,	498	
		5,036
Taxes connected with police courts rather than with police:—		
Fines and penalties from police courts,	3,074	
Fees from police courts,	1,444	
		9,089
Total,		£50,904

The cost of police in Ireland is charged on Imperial not local funds, but there are certain sums produced by local taxation in addition to the foregoing which are applied in aid of the amounts annually voted by Parliament for the maintenance of police.

As regards the Royal Irish Constabulary, payments are only made from local sources to the extent of one-half the cost of an extra force where such is required, and it will be seen by table I. in the appendix that the presentments passed by Grand Juries in 1895 for the maintenance of extra police in counties amounted to £21,811.

The only charge on town rates for police occurs in the cities of Belfast and Londonderry, and in each case it is for one-half the cost of an extra force, and for the discharge of the duties of a night watch performed by the constabulary. The cost of police in those cities is regulated, respectively, by the Acts 28 and 29 Vic., cap. 70, and 33 and 34 Vic., cap. 83, and it amounted in Belfast to £13,310 for the year 1895. The sum of £29 is given under the head of "watching" in the accounts of the City of Londonderry for the same year.

The total charge to local rates in Ireland for the cost of police in 1895 may therefore be set down as amounting possibly to £88,000, while the sums voted by Parliament for the two branches of police service for the year ended in March, 1896, amounted to £1,469,639, viz., £94,178 for the Dublin Metropolitan Police, and £1,375,461 for the Royal Irish Constabulary.

(d.) Taxation in connection with the Port and Docks Board, Dublin.

It is enacted by the Statute 17 Vic., cap. 23, that the cost of preserving and repairing certain quay walls and bridges in the city of Dublin shall be provided by a tax to be levied within the police district of the Metropolis, and by a further Statute, 39 and 40 Vic., cap. lxxxv., that the repayment of a loan obtained thereunder for the erection and maintenance of two new bridges shall be effected by means of a "bridge rate" to be levied upon the "bridge area," which is defined as comprising the Dublin Metropolitan Police District, the portion of the township of New Kilmainham which is not comprised in the Metropolitan Police District, the township of Clontarf, and a part of the county of Dublin as therein described, called the "intermediate district." It is also provided by the latter Act that the bridge rate shall cease to be imposed when the loan obtained for the erection of the bridges referred to shall have been discharged, and that thenceforward the provisions of the first named Act, as above mentioned, shall apply in regard to their maintenance. The two rates in question usually amount to about 2d. in the pound on valuation, and the lodgments made in respect thereof to the credit of the Port and Docks Board during 1895 amounted to £8,742, as may be seen by table IX. of the Appendices.

The loan obtained for the erection of the two bridges amounted to £118,765, of which there had been repaid at the end of 1895 a sum of £79,983.

(e.) Court Leet Presentments.

It has been ascertained that the only Court Leet in Ireland which has not actually ceased to exist is that in the Manor of Killultagh, including the town of Lisburn, but as the taxation formerly imposed by this Court Leet for the maintenance of the old Manor roads is now provided by Grand Jury Cess, and as the markets, reservoirs, water supply, &c., which had been maintained by Court Leet presentments have been sold to the Town Commissioners of Lisburn, the Court has become practically obsolete through disuse.

V.—RECEIPTS OF BURIAL BOARDS.

By Section 160 of the Public Health (Ireland) Act, 1878, 41 & 42 Vic., cap. 52, it is enacted that the Sanitary Authority of each Sanitary District, except towns or townships having Commissioners under local Acts, shall be the burial board for each district, and that the Guardians of the union or unions in which the towns or townships referred to may be situate shall be the burial board in such cases.

The receipts and expenditure of rural and urban burial boards are included, respectively, in those of Boards of Guardians, and in the town returns given herein, and the details of the receipts and expenditure of the burial boards are given in table XI. of the Appendices.

VI.—TAXATION ARISING FROM FEES, STAMPS, FINES, DOGS LICENCE DUTY, &c.

This species of taxation is applied to the remuneration of officers of local courts, and in some instances is applied in aid of Grand Jury Cess and Town Rates, as shown hereinafter.

As regards the officers styled Clerks of the Peace and Clerks of the Crown, whose salaries are charged on local rates, it should be stated that there are now only 14 of the former and 13 of the latter, the County Officers and Courts (Ireland) Act, 1877, having made provision for the uniting of these two offices by His Excellency the Lord Lieutenant when a vacancy occurs in either, and for the appointment to the united office of a person to be styled Clerk of the Crown and Peace, whose salary is paid out of funds provided by Parliament.

(a.) *Clerks of the Peace.*

	£
Salaries and emoluments from Grand Jury cess,	6,919
Fees and emoluments other than from cess or Imperial taxes,	3,415
Received from the Imperial taxes,	1,0[illegible]
Total,	£10,3[illegible]

(b.) *Clerks of the Crown.*

	£
Salaries and other payments from Grand Jury cess,	3,0[illegible]
Emoluments from the Imperial taxes,	1,083
Other emoluments,	310
Total,	£4,[illegible]08

(c.) *Petty Sessions Clerks.*

The receipts from Petty Sessions stamps and Crown fines and the application thereof are shown in the following summary:—

RECEIPTS.	£
Produce of Petty Sessions stamps,	24,111
Produce of Crown fines,	25,845
Dividends,	5,[illegible]1
Amount transferred from Dogs Act fund,	35,180
Total,	£90,[illegible]7

APPLICATION.	£
Officers of local courts,	79,9[illegible]
Treasurers of Boroughs, and private parties,	8,050
Royal Irish Constabulary fund,	1,147
Cattle Disease account,	1[illegible]
Total,	£90,[illegible]4

The salaries and retiring allowances of the clerks of Petty Sessions are charged on the fund produced by Crown fines and the sale of Petty Sessions stamps, and to secure the fund from variation in consequence of fluctuation in the amounts received from these sources, the Registrar of Petty Sessions clerks is authorised by the Act 44 & 45 Vic., cap. 18, to deduct from the Dogs Licence Duty, mentioned in the next section, such sum as the Lord Lieutenant may order for any one year, and to add it to the fund.

(d.) *The Dogs Licence Duty.*

The collection of the dogs licence duty is entrusted to the Petty Sessions clerks, and a return of it is made to Parliament by the Registrar of Petty Sessions clerks, so that an abstract only is given in table XV. A considerable part of the remuneration of Petty Sessions clerks is derived from the dogs licence duty, as mentioned in the preceding section. The surplus of the duty, after providing for the cost of collection is paid over in aid of Grand Jury cess and Town rates.

RECEIPTS.	£
Amount of the Dogs Licence Duty,	41,[illegible]73
Dividends,	[illegible]
	£42,[illegible]

APPLICATION.	£
In aid of Grand Jury cess,	14,[illegible]
In aid of Town rates,	1,[illegible]
Cost of postage, &c.,	54
Deducted and added to Fines and Fees fund, by order of the Lord Lieutenant,	26,439
Total dogs licence duty,	£42,[illegible]

VII.—TAXATION PRODUCED BY TOLLS, DUES, &c.

(a.) Harbour Authorities.

The receipts and expenditure of the Harbour Authorities are shown in the following summary of table XVI :—

Receipts.	£	*Expenditure.*	£
Import and export tonnage and ballast dues,	134,719	New works and improvements,	78,576
Harbour, port, anchorage, buoy, and beaconage tolls,	93,438	Repairs and maintenance of works,	88,859
Pilotage dues,	10,704	Payments in respect of borrowed money,	64,665
Wharf, pier, quay, and dock dues,	80,303	Payments not classed,	65,794
Receipts not classed,	22,477	Interest, annuities, &c.,	102,558
Rents, use of lighter boats, &c.,	65,683	Wages,	33,971
Lighthouse or floating light dues,	616	Salaries,	62,165
Sale of materials,	1,439	Plant, such as dredgers, barges, beacons, &c.,	9,789
Money borrowed on bond,	73,946	Lighting harbours, docks, &c.,	8,537
From the Imperial taxes,	18,116	Rents, rates, taxes, &c.,	14,486
From Grand Jury cess, or other local tax,	2,616	Law expenses,	1,383
		Repayments through Treasury to Imperial taxes,	—
		Lighthouses and floating lights,	3,047
		Repayments to Grand Jury cess,	—
Total receipts,	£409,817	Total expenditure,	£491,880

(b.) Inland Navigations.

(1.) *Maintained out of Grand Jury Cess.*

Receipts.	£	*Expenditure.*	£
From Grand Jury cess,	3,840	Works,	1,369
Tolls,	319	Salaries and incidentals,	640
Other receipts,	73		
Total receipts,	£4,232	Total expenditure,	£2,009

(2.) *Maintained out of the Imperial taxes, or by receipts from Tolls, &c.*

Receipts.	£	*Expenditure.*	£
Parliamentary grant,	603	Works,	3,183
Tolls,	3,231	Salaries and incidentals,	2,018
Receipts not classed,	2,359		
Total receipts,	£6,193	Total expenditure,	£5,197

VIII.—RECEIPTS ON ACCOUNT OF MERCANTILE MARINE FUND.

The following is a summary of the receipts on account of the Mercantile Marine Fund given in table XX :—

	£	£
Light dues,		16,876
Fees under Merchant Shipping Act, viz. :—		
On examination of masters and mates,	227	
On renewal of certificates,	8	
In respect of the survey of vessels,	2,516	
		2,751
Total,		£19,627

Arterial Drainage.

Repayments for Expenditure on Drainage Works executed by Commissioners of Public Works.

The particulars of these repayments have been supplied by the Commissioners of Public Works. The repayments made by proprietors of lands amounted to £33,771 and the sum repaid out of county cess was £1,751, as may be seen by table XIX. on pages 50 and 53.

Loans outstanding against local authorities.

Table XXII. on pages 54 to 57 gives the amount due on account of loans by the several town and harbour authorities, joint burial boards, and the Belfast City and District Water Commissioners at the close of the financial year ended in 1895, with the rate of interest payable in each case.

The loans due by Boards of Guardians on the 29th of September of that year will be found summarized at page 21 of the 24th Report of the Local Government Board, and shown in detail in the Appendix thereto at pages 227 to 286.

The following is a summary of the amount due in respect of loans by each class of local authority named in Table XXII., and by Boards of Guardians.

—	[illegible]	[illegible]	[illegible]	[illegible]	[illegible]	[illegible]	[illegible]	Boards of Guardians.	Total.
1.	2.	3.	4.	5.	6.	7.	8.	9.	10.
[illegible]	£	£	£	£	£	£	£	£	£
	[illegible]	[illegible]	[illegible]	[illegible]	[illegible]	[illegible]	[illegible]	[illegible]	[illegible]

In addition to the debts of harbour authorities given in column 6 of this table, sums amounting to £13,896 remained due on account of loans advanced to Grand Juries for harbour purposes. The amount due by Boards of Guardians given in column 9, includes £25,658, which will not become payable until the 1st of August, 1897, this amount being the second instalment of the loan advanced under the Seed Potatoes Supply (Ireland) Act, 1895.

Note.—Deductions on account of duplicate entries, &c.

In the case of Grand Jury taxation the other receipts given on page 10 have been reduced by £14,588, received from the Dogs licence duty, in that of Union taxation the other receipts of Board of Guardians on page 12 have been reduced by £6,769 on account of duplicate entries, and £4,168 received as repayment of relief, while as regards town taxation the other receipts on page 16, viz., £916,924, have been reduced by the following sums:—£5,929 received from Petty Sessions Stamps and Crown fines, £1,285 from the Dogs licence duty, £1,746 from grants or contributions made for specific purposes, and sums amounting to £22,293 which appear twice in the accounts of local bodies, thereby reducing the amount of such receipts to £185,674.

1.—Summary of Grand Jury Cess authorised to be levied in the year 18[illegible] in each County, and County of [illegible] of Grand Juries, and by the City Accountant, or Borough Treasurer.

Counties and Counties of Cities and of Towns (a.)	Roads and Bridges. New.	Roads and Bridges. Repairs.	[illegible]	[illegible]	Public Buildings. [illegible]	Public Buildings. Other [illegible]	Public Buildings. [illegible]	[illegible]	[illegible]
1	2	3	4	5	6	7	8	9	10
	£	£	£	£	£	£	£	£	£
Antrim,	[illegible]	[illegible]	[illegible]	[illegible]	[illegible]	–	[illegible]	[illegible]	[illegible]
Armagh,	[illegible]	[illegible]	[illegible]	[illegible]	[illegible]	–	[illegible]	[illegible]	[illegible]
Carlow,	–	[illegible]	[illegible]	[illegible]	[illegible]	–	[illegible]	[illegible]	[illegible]
Carrickfergus, Co. of the Town,	[illegible]	[illegible]	–	[illegible]	–	–	[illegible]	[illegible]	[illegible]
Cavan,	[illegible]	[illegible]	[illegible]	[illegible]	[illegible]	–	[illegible]	[illegible]	[illegible]
Clare,	[illegible]	[illegible]	[illegible]	[illegible]	[illegible]	–	[illegible]	[illegible]	[illegible]
Cork,	[illegible]	[illegible]	[illegible]	[illegible]	[illegible]	[illegible]	[illegible]	[illegible]	[illegible]
Cork, County of the City,	–	–	[illegible]	[illegible]	[illegible]	–	[illegible]	[illegible]	[illegible]
Donegal,	[illegible]	[illegible]	[illegible]	[illegible]	[illegible]	–	[illegible]	[illegible]	[illegible]
Down,	[illegible]	[illegible]	[illegible]	[illegible]	[illegible]	–	[illegible]	[illegible]	[illegible]
Drogheda, County of the Town,	[illegible]	[illegible]	[illegible]	[illegible]	[illegible]	[illegible]	[illegible]	[illegible]	[illegible]
Dublin,	[illegible]	[illegible]	–	[illegible]	[illegible]	–	[illegible]	[illegible]	[illegible]
Dublin, County of the City,	–	–	[illegible]	[illegible]	[illegible]	[illegible]	–	[illegible]	[illegible]
Fermanagh,	[illegible]	[illegible]	[illegible]	[illegible]	[illegible]	–	[illegible]	[illegible]	[illegible]
Galway,	[illegible]	[illegible]	[illegible]	[illegible]	[illegible]	–	[illegible]	[illegible]	[illegible]
Galway, County of the Town,	–	[illegible]	–	[illegible]	–	–	[illegible]	[illegible]	[illegible]
Kerry,	[illegible]	[illegible]	[illegible]	[illegible]	[illegible]	–	[illegible]	[illegible]	[illegible]
Kildare,	[illegible]	[illegible]	[illegible]	[illegible]	[illegible]	–	[illegible]	[illegible]	[illegible]
Kilkenny,	–	[illegible]	[illegible]	[illegible]	[illegible]	–	[illegible]	[illegible]	[illegible]
Kilkenny, County of the City,	[illegible]	[illegible]	[illegible]	[illegible]	[illegible]	–	[illegible]	[illegible]	[illegible]
King's County,	[illegible]	[illegible]	[illegible]	[illegible]	[illegible]	–	[illegible]	[illegible]	[illegible]
Leitrim,	[illegible]	[illegible]	[illegible]	[illegible]	[illegible]	–	[illegible]	[illegible]	[illegible]
Limerick,	[illegible]	[illegible]	[illegible]	[illegible]	[illegible]	–	[illegible]	[illegible]	[illegible]
Limerick, County of the City,	–	–	[illegible]	[illegible]	[illegible]	–	[illegible]	[illegible]	[illegible]
Londonderry,	[illegible]	[illegible]	[illegible]	[illegible]	[illegible]	–	[illegible]	[illegible]	[illegible]
Longford,	[illegible]	[illegible]	[illegible]	[illegible]	[illegible]	–	[illegible]	[illegible]	[illegible]
Louth,	[illegible]	[illegible]	[illegible]	[illegible]	[illegible]	–	[illegible]	[illegible]	[illegible]
Mayo,	[illegible]	[illegible]	[illegible]	[illegible]	[illegible]	–	[illegible]	[illegible]	[illegible]
Meath,	[illegible]	[illegible]	[illegible]	[illegible]	[illegible]	–	[illegible]	[illegible]	[illegible]
Monaghan,	[illegible]	[illegible]	[illegible]	[illegible]	[illegible]	–	[illegible]	[illegible]	[illegible]
Queen's County,	[illegible]	[illegible]	[illegible]	[illegible]	[illegible]	[illegible]	[illegible]	[illegible]	[illegible]
Roscommon,	[illegible]	[illegible]	[illegible]	[illegible]	[illegible]	–	[illegible]	[illegible]	[illegible]
Sligo,	[illegible]	[illegible]	[illegible]	[illegible]	[illegible]	–	[illegible]	[illegible]	[illegible]
Tipperary, North Riding,	[illegible]	[illegible]	[illegible]	[illegible]	[illegible]	–	[illegible]	[illegible]	[illegible]
Tipperary, South Riding,	[illegible]	[illegible]	[illegible]	[illegible]	[illegible]	–	[illegible]	[illegible]	[illegible]
Tyrone,	[illegible]	[illegible]	[illegible]	[illegible]	[illegible]	–	[illegible]	[illegible]	[illegible]
Waterford,	[illegible]	[illegible]	[illegible]	[illegible]	[illegible]	–	[illegible]	[illegible]	[illegible]
Waterford, County of the City,	[illegible]	[illegible]	[illegible]	[illegible]	[illegible]	–	–	[illegible]	[illegible]
Westmeath,	[illegible]	[illegible]	[illegible]	[illegible]	[illegible]	–	[illegible]	[illegible]	[illegible]
Wexford,	[illegible]	[illegible]	[illegible]	[illegible]	[illegible]	–	–	[illegible]	[illegible]
Wicklow,	[illegible]	[illegible]	[illegible]	[illegible]	[illegible]	–	[illegible]	[illegible]	[illegible]
Total,	[illegible]	[illegible]	[illegible]	[illegible]	[illegible]	[illegible]	[illegible]	[illegible]	[illegible]

of a city and County of a town, compiled from returns furnished by County Treasurers, Secretaries in the cases of the Counties of the cities of Cork, Dublin, and Limerick.

[illegible] 11	[illegible] 12	[illegible] 13	[illegible] 14	[illegible] 15	[illegible] 16	[illegible] 17	[illegible] 18	[illegible] 19	[illegible] 20	[illegible] 21	COUNTIES AND COUNTIES OF CITIES AND OF TOWNS. (a.) 22
£	£	£	£	£	£	£	£	£	s. d.	s. d.	
[illegible]	[illegible]	[illegible]	[illegible]	775	[illegible]	[illegible]	[illegible]	[illegible]	[illegible]	[illegible]	Antrim.
[illegible]	[illegible]	[illegible]	-	[illegible]	[illegible]	[illegible]	[illegible]	[illegible]	[illegible]	[illegible]	Armagh.
11	[illegible]	[illegible]	-	[illegible]	[illegible]	[illegible]	[illegible]	11,[illegible]	[illegible]	[illegible]	Carlow.
-	[illegible]	[illegible]	-	6	271	[illegible]	5	[illegible]	[illegible]	[illegible]	Carrickfergus, Co. of the Town.
-	[illegible]	[illegible]	-	[illegible]	[illegible]	[illegible]	[illegible]	[illegible]	[illegible]	[illegible]	Cavan.
[illegible]	[illegible]	[illegible]	-	[illegible]	[illegible]	[illegible]	[illegible]	[illegible]	[illegible]	[illegible]	Clare.
[illegible]	[illegible]	[illegible]	-	[illegible]	[illegible]	[illegible]	[illegible]	[illegible]	[illegible]	[illegible]	Cork.
-	[illegible]	[illegible]	-	[illegible]	[illegible]	[illegible]	[illegible]	[illegible]	[illegible]	[illegible]	Cork, County of the City.
-	[illegible]	[illegible]	-	[illegible]	[illegible]	[illegible]	[illegible]	[illegible]	[illegible]	[illegible]	Donegal.
[illegible]	[illegible]	[illegible]	[illegible]	[illegible]	[illegible]	[illegible]	[illegible]	[illegible]	[illegible]	[illegible]	Down.
-	[illegible]	[illegible]	-	[illegible]	[illegible]	[illegible]	[illegible]	[illegible]	[illegible]	[illegible]	Drogheda, County of the Town.
[illegible]	[illegible]	[illegible]	-	[illegible]	[illegible]	[illegible]	[illegible]	[illegible]	[illegible]	[illegible]	Dublin.
-	[illegible]	[illegible]	-	-	[illegible]	[illegible]	[illegible]	[illegible]	[illegible]	[illegible]	Dublin, County of the City.
-	[illegible]	[illegible]	-	[illegible]	[illegible]	[illegible]	[illegible]	[illegible]	[illegible]	[illegible]	Fermanagh.
[illegible]	[illegible]	[illegible]	-	[illegible]	[illegible]	[illegible]	[illegible]	[illegible]	[illegible]	[illegible]	Galway.
-	[illegible]	[illegible]	-	[illegible]	[illegible]	[illegible]	[illegible]	[illegible]	[illegible]	[illegible]	Galway, County of the Town.
[illegible]	[illegible]	[illegible]	-	[illegible]	[illegible]	[illegible]	[illegible]	[illegible]	[illegible]	[illegible]	Kerry.
[illegible]	[illegible]	[illegible]	-	[illegible]	[illegible]	[illegible]	[illegible]	[illegible]	[illegible]	[illegible]	Kildare.
-	[illegible]	[illegible]	-	[illegible]	[illegible]	[illegible]	[illegible]	[illegible]	[illegible]	[illegible]	Kilkenny.
[illegible]	[illegible]	[illegible]	-	[illegible]	[illegible]	[illegible]	[illegible]	[illegible]	[illegible]	[illegible]	Kilkenny, County of the City.
-	[illegible]	[illegible]	-	[illegible]	[illegible]	[illegible]	[illegible]	[illegible]	[illegible]	[illegible]	King's County.
-	[illegible]	[illegible]	-	[illegible]	[illegible]	[illegible]	[illegible]	[illegible]	[illegible]	[illegible]	Leitrim.
[illegible]	[illegible]	[illegible]	-	[illegible]	[illegible]	[illegible]	[illegible]	[illegible]	[illegible]	[illegible]	Limerick.
-	[illegible]	[illegible]	-	[illegible]	[illegible]	[illegible]	[illegible]	[illegible]	[illegible]	[illegible]	Limerick, County of the City.
-	[illegible]	[illegible]	-	[illegible]	[illegible]	[illegible]	[illegible]	[illegible]	[illegible]	[illegible]	Londonderry.
-	[illegible]	[illegible]	-	[illegible]	[illegible]	[illegible]	[illegible]	[illegible]	[illegible]	[illegible]	Longford.
-	[illegible]	[illegible]	-	[illegible]	[illegible]	[illegible]	[illegible]	[illegible]	[illegible]	[illegible]	Louth.
-	[illegible]	[illegible]	-	[illegible]	[illegible]	[illegible]	[illegible]	[illegible]	[illegible]	[illegible]	Mayo.
-	[illegible]	[illegible]	-	[illegible]	[illegible]	[illegible]	[illegible]	[illegible]	[illegible]	[illegible]	Meath.
-	[illegible]	[illegible]	-	[illegible]	[illegible]	[illegible]	[illegible]	[illegible]	[illegible]	[illegible]	Monaghan.
-	[illegible]	[illegible]	-	[illegible]	[illegible]	[illegible]	[illegible]	[illegible]	[illegible]	[illegible]	Queen's County.
[illegible]	[illegible]	[illegible]	-	[illegible]	[illegible]	[illegible]	[illegible]	[illegible]	[illegible]	[illegible]	Roscommon.
-	[illegible]	[illegible]	-	[illegible]	[illegible]	[illegible]	[illegible]	[illegible]	[illegible]	[illegible]	Sligo.
[illegible]	[illegible]	[illegible]	-	[illegible]	[illegible]	[illegible]	[illegible]	[illegible]	[illegible]	[illegible]	Tipperary, North Riding.
[illegible]	[illegible]	[illegible]	-	[illegible]	[illegible]	[illegible]	[illegible]	[illegible]	[illegible]	[illegible]	Tipperary, South Riding.
[illegible]	[illegible]	[illegible]	-	[illegible]	[illegible]	[illegible]	[illegible]	[illegible]	[illegible]	[illegible]	Tyrone.
[illegible]	[illegible]	[illegible]	-	[illegible]	[illegible]	[illegible]	[illegible]	[illegible]	[illegible]	[illegible]	Waterford.
-	[illegible]	[illegible]	[illegible]	[illegible]	[illegible]	[illegible]	[illegible]	[illegible]	[illegible]	[illegible]	Waterford, County of the City.
-	[illegible]	[illegible]	-	[illegible]	[illegible]	[illegible]	[illegible]	[illegible]	[illegible]	[illegible]	Westmeath.
[illegible]	[illegible]	[illegible]	-	[illegible]	[illegible]	[illegible]	[illegible]	[illegible]	[illegible]	[illegible]	Wexford.
-	[illegible]	[illegible]	-	[illegible]	[illegible]	[illegible]	[illegible]	[illegible]	[illegible]	[illegible]	Wicklow.

II.—SUMMARY, showing the amount of Grand Jury Cess, and other receipts, in each County by the Auditors of the

[illegible]	Receipts.										
	[illegible]	[illegible]	[illegible]	[illegible]	[illegible]	[illegible]	[illegible]	[illegible]	[illegible]	[illegible]	[illegible]
1.	2.	3.	4.	5.	6.	7.	8.	9.	10.	11.	12.
	£	£	£	£	£	£	£	£	£	£	£
Antrim,	[illegible]	[illegible]	[illegible]	—	[illegible]	[illegible]	[illegible]	[illegible]	[illegible]	—	[illegible]
Armagh,	[illegible]	[illegible]	[illegible]	—	[illegible]	[illegible]	—	[illegible]	[illegible]	—	[illegible]
Carlow,	[illegible]	[illegible]	[illegible]	—	[illegible]	[illegible]	—	[illegible]	[illegible]	—	[illegible]
Carrickfergus, Co. of the Town,	[illegible]	[illegible]	[illegible]	—	[illegible]	—	[illegible]	[illegible]	[illegible]	—	[illegible]
Cavan,	[illegible]	[illegible]	[illegible]	[illegible]	[illegible]	—	—	[illegible]	[illegible]	—	[illegible]
Clare,	[illegible]	[illegible]	[illegible]	[illegible]	[illegible]	—	—	[illegible]	[illegible]	—	[illegible]
Cork,	[illegible]	[illegible]	[illegible]	[illegible]	[illegible]	[illegible]	—	[illegible]	[illegible]	—	[illegible]
Donegal,	[illegible]	[illegible]	[illegible]	[illegible]	[illegible]	—	—	[illegible]	[illegible]	—	[illegible]
Down,	[illegible]	[illegible]	[illegible]	—	[illegible]	[illegible]	—	[illegible]	[illegible]	—	[illegible]
Drogheda, Co. of the Town,	[illegible]	[illegible]	[illegible]	—	—	[illegible]	[illegible]	[illegible]	[illegible]	—	[illegible]
Dublin County,	[illegible]	[illegible]	[illegible]	[illegible]	[illegible]	—	—	[illegible]	[illegible]	—	[illegible]
Fermanagh,	[illegible]	[illegible]	[illegible]	[illegible]	[illegible]	—	—	[illegible]	[illegible]	—	[illegible]
Galway,	[illegible]	[illegible]	[illegible]	[illegible]	[illegible]	—	[illegible]	[illegible]	[illegible]	—	[illegible]
Galway, Co. of the Town,	[illegible]	[illegible]	[illegible]	—	[illegible]	—	—	[illegible]	[illegible]	—	[illegible]
Kerry,	[illegible]	[illegible]	[illegible]	[illegible]	—	[illegible]	—	[illegible]	[illegible]	—	[illegible]
Kildare,	[illegible]	[illegible]	[illegible]	—	[illegible]	—	—	[illegible]	[illegible]	—	[illegible]
Kilkenny,	[illegible]	[illegible]	[illegible]	—	[illegible]		—	[illegible]	[illegible]	—	[illegible]
Kilkenny, Co. of the City,	[illegible]	[illegible]	[illegible]	—	[illegible]	—	—	[illegible]	[illegible]	—	[illegible]
King's County,	[illegible]	[illegible]	[illegible]	—	[illegible]	[illegible]	—	[illegible]	[illegible]	—	[illegible]
Leitrim,	[illegible]	[illegible]	[illegible]	[illegible]	[illegible]	—	—	[illegible]	[illegible]	—	[illegible]
Limerick,	[illegible]	[illegible]	[illegible]	—	[illegible]	—	—	[illegible]	[illegible]	—	[illegible]
Londonderry,	[illegible]	[illegible]	[illegible]	—	—	—	—	[illegible]	[illegible]	—	[illegible]
Longford,	[illegible]	[illegible]	[illegible]	—	[illegible]	—	—	[illegible]	[illegible]	—	[illegible]
Louth,	[illegible]	[illegible]	[illegible]	—	[illegible]	[illegible]	—	[illegible]	[illegible]	—	[illegible]
Mayo,	[illegible]	[illegible]	[illegible]	[illegible]	[illegible]	—	—	[illegible]	[illegible]	—	[illegible]
Meath,	[illegible]	[illegible]	[illegible]	—	[illegible]	—	—	[illegible]	[illegible]	—	[illegible]
Monaghan,	—	[illegible]	[illegible]	—	[illegible]	—	—	[illegible]	[illegible]	—	[illegible]
Queen's County,	[illegible]	[illegible]	[illegible]	—	[illegible]	[illegible]	[illegible]	[illegible]	[illegible]	—	[illegible]
Roscommon,	[illegible]	[illegible]	[illegible]	—	[illegible]	[illegible]	—	[illegible]	[illegible]	—	[illegible]
Sligo,	[illegible]	[illegible]	[illegible]	—	[illegible]	[illegible]	[illegible]	[illegible]	[illegible]	—	[illegible]
Tipperary, North Riding,	[illegible]	[illegible]	[illegible]	—	[illegible]	[illegible]	—	[illegible]	[illegible]	—	[illegible]
Tipperary, South Riding,	[illegible]	[illegible]	[illegible]	—	[illegible]	[illegible]	—	[illegible]	[illegible]	—	[illegible]
Tyrone,	[illegible]	[illegible]	[illegible]	[illegible]	[illegible]	—	—	[illegible]	[illegible]	—	[illegible]
Waterford,	[illegible]	[illegible]	[illegible]	—	[illegible]	—	—	[illegible]	[illegible]	—	[illegible]
* Waterford, County of the City,	[illegible]	[illegible]	[illegible]	—	—	—	—	[illegible]	[illegible]	[illegible]	[illegible]
Westmeath,	[illegible]	[illegible]	[illegible]	—	[illegible]	—	—	[illegible]	[illegible]	—	[illegible]

during the year 18[illegible], with the expenditure thereof, prepared from the abstracts furnished [illegible] Local Government Board.

[illegible]	[illegible]	[illegible]	[illegible]	[illegible]	[illegible]	[illegible]	[illegible]	[illegible]	[illegible]
[illegible]	[illegible]	[illegible]	[illegible]	[illegible]	[illegible]	[illegible]	[illegible]	[illegible]	[illegible]
£	£	£	£	£	£	£	£	£	
—	[illegible]	[illegible]	[illegible]	—	—	[illegible]	[illegible]	[illegible]	Antrim.
—	[illegible]	[illegible]	—	—	—	[illegible]	[illegible]	[illegible]	Armagh.
—	[illegible]	[illegible]	—	—	—	[illegible]	[illegible]	[illegible]	Carlow.
—	[illegible]	1	—	—	—	[illegible]	[illegible]	[illegible]	Carrickfergus, Co. of the Town.
—	[illegible]	[illegible]	—	[illegible]	—	[illegible]	[illegible]	[illegible]	Cavan.
—	[illegible]	[illegible]	—	—	[illegible]	[illegible]	[illegible]	[illegible]	Clare.
—	[illegible]	[illegible]	—	—	—	[illegible]	[illegible]	[illegible]	Cork.
—	[illegible]	[illegible]	—	—	—	[illegible]	[illegible]	[illegible]	Donegal.
—	[illegible]	[illegible]	[illegible]	—	—	[illegible]	[illegible]	[illegible]	Down.
—	[illegible]	[illegible]	[illegible]	—	—	[illegible]	[illegible]	[illegible]	Drogheda, Co. of the Town.
—	[illegible]	[illegible]	—	[illegible]	[illegible]	[illegible]	[illegible]	[illegible]	Dublin County.
—	[illegible]	[illegible]	—	—	—	[illegible]	[illegible]	[illegible]	Fermanagh.
—	[illegible]	[illegible]	[illegible]	[illegible]	[illegible]	[illegible]	[illegible]	[illegible]	Galway.
—	[illegible]	[illegible]	—	—	—	[illegible]	[illegible]	[illegible]	Galway, Co. of the Town.
—	[illegible]	[illegible]	—	—	—	[illegible]	[illegible]	[illegible]	Kerry.
—	[illegible]	[illegible]	—	—	[illegible]	[illegible]	[illegible]	[illegible]	Kildare.
—	[illegible]	[illegible]	—	—	[illegible]	[illegible]	[illegible]	[illegible]	Kilkenny.
—	[illegible]	[illegible]	—	—	—	[illegible]	[illegible]	[illegible]	Kilkenny, Co. of the City.
—	[illegible]	[illegible]	—	—	—	[illegible]	[illegible]	[illegible]	King's County.
—	[illegible]	[illegible]	—	—	—	[illegible]	[illegible]	[illegible]	Leitrim.
—	[illegible]	[illegible]	—	—	[illegible]	[illegible]	[illegible]	[illegible]	Limerick.
—	[illegible]	[illegible]	[illegible]	—	—	[illegible]	[illegible]	[illegible]	Londonderry.
—	[illegible]	[illegible]	—	—	[illegible]	[illegible]	[illegible]	[illegible]	Longford.
—	[illegible]	[illegible]	—	—	[illegible]	[illegible]	[illegible]	[illegible]	Louth.
—	[illegible]	[illegible]	—	[illegible]	[illegible]	[illegible]	[illegible]	[illegible]	Mayo.
—	[illegible]	[illegible]	—	—	—	[illegible]	[illegible]	[illegible]	Meath.
[illegible]	[illegible]	[illegible]	—	—	—	[illegible]	[illegible]	[illegible]	Monaghan.
—	[illegible]	[illegible]	[illegible]	—	[illegible]	[illegible]	[illegible]	[illegible]	Queen's County.
—	[illegible]	[illegible]	—	—	—	[illegible]	[illegible]	[illegible]	Roscommon.
—	[illegible]	[illegible]	—	—	—	[illegible]	[illegible]	[illegible]	Sligo.
—	[illegible]	[illegible]	[illegible]	—	—	[illegible]	[illegible]	[illegible]	Tipperary, North Riding.
	[illegible]	[illegible]		—	[illegible]	[illegible]	[illegible]	[illegible]	Tipperary, South Riding.
—	[illegible]	[illegible]	—	—	[illegible]	[illegible]	[illegible]	[illegible]	Tyrone.
—	[illegible]	[illegible]	—	—	—	[illegible]	[illegible]	[illegible]	Waterford.
—	[illegible]	[illegible]	—	—	—	[illegible]	—	[illegible]	Waterford, Co. of the City.
—	[illegible]	[illegible]	—	—	—	[illegible]	[illegible]	[illegible]	Westmeath.

III.—POOR RATE.—The SUMMARY STATEMENT of the receipts and

IV.—TOWN COUNCILS.—SUMMARY STATEMENT showing the receipts

(Note.—[illegible])

RECEIPTS.

Cities and Corporate Towns, arranged in Provinces. (1)	Balance in favour of the Council at the commencement of the year.	Receipts: [illegible]	[illegible]	[illegible]	[illegible]	[illegible]	[illegible]	[illegible]	[illegible]	[illegible]
	£	£	£	£	£	£	£	£	£	£
LEINSTER.										
Drogheda,	–	–	–	–	–	–	41	[illegible]	[illegible]	–
Dublin,	[illegible]	–	[illegible]	–	[illegible]	[illegible]	[illegible]	[illegible]	[illegible]	[illegible]
Kilkenny,	–	–	–	–	–	–	73	–	[illegible]	–
Wexford,	[illegible]	[illegible]	[illegible]	–	[illegible]	–	113	61	[illegible]	–
MUNSTER.										
Clonmel,	–	[illegible]	[illegible]	–	–	–	[illegible]	–	[illegible]	–
Cork,	[illegible]	[illegible]	[illegible]	–	[illegible]	[illegible]	[illegible]	–	[illegible]	[illegible]
Limerick,	–	–	[illegible]	–	–	[illegible]	[illegible]		[illegible]	–
Waterford,	–	–	–	–	[illegible]	–	[illegible]	–	[illegible]	[illegible]
ULSTER.										
Belfast,	[illegible]	[illegible]	[illegible]	–	[illegible]	–	[illegible]	[illegible]	[illegible]	–
Londonderry,	–	–	[illegible]	–	–	–	[illegible]	–	[illegible]	–
CONNAUGHT.										
Sligo,	–	[illegible]	–	–	[illegible]	–	[illegible]	–	[illegible]	–
Total, 18[illegible],	[illegible]	[illegible]	[illegible]	–	[illegible]	[illegible]	[illegible]	[illegible]	[illegible]	[illegible]
" 18[illegible],	[illegible]	[illegible]	[illegible]	–	[illegible]	[illegible]	[illegible]	[illegible]	[illegible]	[illegible]
Increase,	[illegible]	–	–	–	[illegible]	–	[illegible]	–	–	–
Decrease,	–	[illegible]	[illegible]	–	–	[illegible]	–	[illegible]	[illegible]	75

EXPENDITURE.

Cities and Corporate Towns, arranged in Provinces.	Balance against the Council at the commencement of the year.	Expenditure: Improvement of Town by building, &c.	Paving and repair of streets.	Cleansing and watering streets.	Lighting, including lamps, pipes, &c.	Watching.	Water supply.	Constructing, repairing, or cleansing sewers, &c.
	£	£	£	£	£	£	£	£
LEINSTER.								
Drogheda,	[illegible]	[illegible]	[illegible]	[illegible]	[illegible]	[illegible]	[illegible]	[illegible]
Dublin,	–	[illegible]	[illegible]	[illegible]	[illegible]	–	[illegible]	[illegible]
Kilkenny,	[illegible]	–	171	[illegible]	[illegible]	[illegible]	[illegible]	[illegible]
Wexford,	–	–	[illegible]	[illegible]	[illegible]	–	[illegible]	[illegible]
MUNSTER.								
Clonmel,	[illegible]	–	[illegible]	–	[illegible]	–	[illegible]	–
Cork,	–	[illegible]	[illegible]	[illegible]	[illegible]	–	[illegible]	[illegible]
Limerick,	[illegible]	[illegible]	[illegible]	[illegible]	[illegible]	[illegible]	[illegible]	[illegible]
Waterford,	[illegible]	[illegible]	[illegible]	[illegible]	[illegible]	–	[illegible]	[illegible]
ULSTER.								
Belfast,	–	[illegible]	[illegible]	[illegible]	[illegible]	[illegible]	–	[illegible]
Londonderry,	[illegible]	–	[illegible]	[illegible]	[illegible]	[illegible]	[illegible]	[illegible]
CONNAUGHT.								
Sligo,	[illegible]	–	[illegible]	[illegible]	[illegible]	[illegible]	[illegible]	[illegible]
Total, 18[illegible],	[illegible]	[illegible]	[illegible]	[illegible]	[illegible]	[illegible]	[illegible]	[illegible]
" 18[illegible],	[illegible]	[illegible]	[illegible]	[illegible]	[illegible]	[illegible]	[illegible]	[illegible]
Increase,	–	–	[illegible]	[illegible]	–	–	–	–
Decrease,	[illegible]	[illegible]	–	–	[illegible]	[illegible]	[illegible]	[illegible]

expenditure of Boards of Guardians will be found on page 12.

and expenditure of Town Councils during the financial year ended in 1895.

[illegible]

Receipts.

Revenue.					[illegible]	Total.	Cities and Corporate Towns, arranged in Provinces. (B.)
[illegible]	[illegible]	[illegible]	Other receipts.	Total receipts.			
£	£	£	£	£	£	£	LEINSTER.
-	4,6[illegible]	-	[illegible]	[illegible]	1,377	6,717	Drogheda.
[illegible]	77,154	42,[illegible]	[illegible]	[illegible]	[illegible]	[illegible]	Dublin.
-	2,[illegible]	-	[illegible]	[illegible]	4,731	[illegible]	Kilkenny.
-	[illegible]	-	[illegible]	6,7[illegible]	-	6,1[illegible]	Wexford.
							MUNSTER.
[illegible]	[illegible]	-	[illegible]	4,[illegible]	[illegible]	[illegible]	Clonmel.
-	[illegible]	[illegible]	[illegible]	[illegible]	[illegible]	[illegible]	Cork.
-	[illegible]	7,[illegible]	[illegible]	[illegible]	[illegible]	[illegible]	Limerick.
-	[illegible]	1,[illegible]	1,073	19,[illegible]	6,[illegible]	[illegible]	Waterford.
							ULSTER.
-	[illegible]	171,[illegible]	[illegible]	[illegible]	-	[illegible]	Belfast.
-	[illegible]	1,[illegible]	[illegible]	[illegible]	4,[illegible]	[illegible]	Londonderry.
							CONNAUGHT.
-	[illegible]	[illegible]	1,[illegible]	[illegible]	[illegible]	[illegible]	Sligo.
[illegible]	[illegible]	[illegible]	[illegible]	[illegible]	[illegible]	[illegible]	Total, 1895.
[illegible]	[illegible]	[illegible]	[illegible]	[illegible]	[illegible]	[illegible]	" 1894.
-	[illegible]	-	[illegible]	-	[illegible]	-	Increase.
[illegible]	-	[illegible]		[illegible]		[illegible]	Decrease.

Expenditure.

[illegible]					[illegible]	Total.	Cities and Corporate Towns, arranged in Provinces.
[illegible]	[illegible]	[illegible]	Other expenses.	Total expenditure.			
£	£	£	£	£	£	£	LEINSTER.
[illegible]	-	[illegible]	[illegible]	[illegible]	-	[illegible]	Drogheda.
[illegible]	17,[illegible]	[illegible]	[illegible]	[illegible]	-	[illegible]	Dublin.
[illegible]	-	[illegible]	[illegible]	[illegible]	-	[illegible]	Kilkenny.
[illegible]	[illegible]	1,[illegible]	[illegible]	[illegible]	1,[illegible]	[illegible]	Wexford.
							MUNSTER.
[illegible]	[illegible]	[illegible]	1,[illegible]	[illegible]	-	4,7[illegible]	Clonmel.
[illegible]	[illegible]	[illegible]	[illegible]	[illegible]	-	[illegible]	Cork.
[illegible]	[illegible]	[illegible]	[illegible]	[illegible]	-	[illegible]	Limerick.
[illegible]	-	[illegible]	[illegible]	[illegible]	-	[illegible]	Waterford.
							ULSTER.
[illegible]	7,[illegible]	[illegible]	[illegible]	[illegible]	[illegible]	[illegible]	Belfast.
[illegible]	-	[illegible]	[illegible]	[illegible]	-	[illegible]	Londonderry.
							CONNAUGHT.
[illegible]	[illegible]	[illegible]	[illegible]	[illegible]	-	[illegible]	Sligo.
[illegible]	[illegible]	[illegible]	[illegible]	[illegible]	[illegible]	[illegible]	Total, 1895.
[illegible]	[illegible]	[illegible]	[illegible]	[illegible]	[illegible]	[illegible]	" 1894.
[illegible]	[illegible]	-	[illegible]	-	-	-	Increase.
-	-	[illegible]	-	[illegible]	[illegible]	[illegible]	Decrease.

V.—TOWN COMMISSIONERS UNDER ACT OF 1854. SUMMARY of Returns of Receipts and Expenditure of financial year

Towns, arranged in Counties and Provinces. *(28.)	Balance in favour at the commencement of the year	Rates for general purposes	[illegible]	Other Rates	Fees [illegible]	Town Property, Markets & Houses	Borrowed on security of Rates	[illegible]	[illegible]	Other Receipts	Total Receipts	Balance [illegible] at the end of the year	Total	[illegible]
LEINSTER.	£	£	£	£	£	£	£	£	£	£	£	£	£	£
Carlow:														
Bagenalstown,	51	109	-	-	-	-	-	-	-	24	133	-	143	-
Carlow,	2,043	1,525	-	-	393	43	7,780	63	148	101	9,199	376	11,589	-
Dublin:														
Balbriggan,	29	94	-	-	-	15	-	-	-	14	123	-	152	-
Killiney and Ballybrack,	418	1,578	-	-	-	73	-	-	87	655	2,393	-	2,822	-
Kildare:														
Athy,	-	161	-	-	97	6	-	80	-	24	271	-	271	76
Naas,	47	158	-	-	90	11	-	-	-	82	341	-	381	-
Newbridge,	130	80	-	-	47	15	-	-	-	46	187	-	317	-
Kilkenny:														
Callan,	93	-	-	-	91	60	-	-	-	95	244	-	336	-
King's:														
Parsonstown,	291	340	-	-	-	-	-	-	11	130	479	-	849	-
Tullamore,	67	245	-	-	-	30	-	-	-	53	326	-	391	-
Longford:														
Granard,	84	16	-	-	65	-	780	-	6	22	884	-	946	-
Longford,	1	308	-	-	-	-	-	-	-	111	419	-	420	-
Louth:														
Ardee,	150	94	-	-	-	97	-	-	-	76	368	-	622	-
Dundalk,	-	6,318	-	-	-	441	500	-	175	1,482	8,895	63	8,958	358
Meath:														
Kells,	79	-	-	-	-	850	-	146	7	84	1,143	-	1,222	-
Navan,	39	309	-	-	22	-	-	-	7	60	371	-	420	-
Trim,	-	77	-	-	19	600	-	-	-	48	744	-	749	177
Queen's:														
Maryborough,	91	180	-	-	-	12	-	-	-	40	232	-	324	-
Mountmellick,	11	140	-	-	-	-	-	-	-	38	178	-	189	-
Westmeath:														
Athlone (pt. in Roscommon),	1,209	419	-	-	217	-	2,130	60	27	391	3,244	146	4,599	-
Mullingar,	189	891	-	-	-	30	500	3	-	181	1,105	-	1,294	-
Wexford:														
Enniscorthy,	71	374	-	-	-	-	350	-	20	175	909	-	980	-
Gorey,	6	209	-	-	95	6	-	110	-	20	391	-	397	-
New Ross (pt. in Kilkenny),	-	349	-	-	-	646	-	403	14	144	1,590	-	1,590	77
Wicklow:														
Arklow,	140	136	-	170	-	-	-	-	-	30	336	-	476	-
Total in Leinster (20),	5,244	14,984	-	170	1,676	2,336	11,480	782	377	3,412	35,191	1,012	40,807	450
MUNSTER.														
Clare:														
Ennis,	40	884	-	146	-	44	-	-	8	644	1,759	-	1,879	-
Kilrush,	-	99	-	-	-	-	-	-	6	80	185	60	245	46
Cork:														
Clonakilty,	-	-	-	-	399	6	-	-	7	230	481	-	481	85
Fermoy,	-	3,571	-	104	-	-	320	146	96	330	3,922	-	4,011	41
Kinsale,	130	484	-	30	60	340	-	30	7	160	861	-	761	-
Youghal,	117	773	-	-	-	-	-	-	-	371	1,144	-	1,261	-
Macroom,	51	284	-	-	-	-	-	-	-	80	364	-	415	-
Queenstown,	-	390	-	2,330	71	-	440	-	390	190	4,337	-	3,317	130
Skibbereen,	122	40	-	-	381	60	-	-	-	42	523	-	595	-
Kerry:														
Killarney,	5	420	-	-	170	-	-	-	31	470	1,120	66	1,420	74
Listowel,	-	1,248	-	-	-	-	-	-	4	90	1,331	440	1,360	-
Tralee,	-	1,397	-	1,100	300	30	-	-	160	2,430	5,340	376	5,600	300
Limerick:														
Rathkeale,	-	311	-	-	44	-	-	-	-	19	374	-	374	34
Tipperary:														
Carrick-on-Suir,	19	361	-	-	-	11	-	-	6	90	637	-	670	-
Cashel,	291	-	-	-	4	1,354	-	-	6	50	1,393	-	1,610	-
Fethard,	740	879	-	-	-	94	-	171	-	71	1,900	-	776	-
Nenagh,	84	280	-	-	-	32	-	-	4	140	890	-	880	-
Templemore,	244	315	-	-	-	-	-	-	69	319	2,871	-	3,321	-
Thurles,	151	430	-	-	-	-	-	-	-	164	331	-	340	-
Tipperary,														
Waterford:														
Dungarvan,	-	730	-	300	60	150	200	60	40	300	2,370	1,320	4,830	300
Lismore,	116	80	-	-	-	-	-	-	-	40	120	-	236	-
Total in Munster (25),	1,812	3,840	-	4,394	2,300	1,800	720	300	500	6,471	27,300	3,400	41,300	1,740

* See note 28.

Town Commissioners under Towns Improvement (Ireland) Act, 1854 (17 and 18 Vic., c. 103) for the [illegible] ended in 1895.

[illegible]	Paving and Cleansing of Streets.	[illegible]	[illegible]	Watching.	Water Supply.	[illegible]	Other Sanitary [illegible]	[illegible]	[illegible]	[illegible]	Total Expenditure.	Balance in Treasury at close of the year.	Total.	Towns, arranged in Counties and Provinces.
£	£	£	£	£	£	£	£	£	£	£	£	£	£	LEINSTER.
														Carlow:
–	–	[illegible]	–	–	–	–	–	–	–	[illegible]	[illegible]	[illegible]	[illegible]	Bagenalstown.
[illegible]	[illegible]	[illegible]	[illegible]	–	[illegible]	–	[illegible]	[illegible]	[illegible]	[illegible]	[illegible]	–	[illegible]	Carlow.
														Dublin:
–	–	[illegible]	–	–	–	–	–	–	[illegible]	[illegible]	[illegible]	[illegible]	[illegible]	Balbriggan.
–	[illegible]	[illegible]	–	–	[illegible]	[illegible]	[illegible]	[illegible]	[illegible]	[illegible]	[illegible]	[illegible]	[illegible]	Killiney and Ballybrack.
														Kildare:
–	[illegible]	[illegible]	[illegible]	–	–	–	–	–	–	[illegible]	[illegible]	[illegible]	[illegible]	Athy.
–	–	[illegible]	–	–	–	–	–	–	–	[illegible]	[illegible]	[illegible]	[illegible]	Naas.
–	[illegible]	[illegible]	–	–	–	–	–	–	–	[illegible]	[illegible]	[illegible]	[illegible]	Newbridge.
														Kilkenny:
–	[illegible]	[illegible]	–	–	–	–	–	–	[illegible]	[illegible]	[illegible]	[illegible]	[illegible]	Callan.
														King's:
–	[illegible]	[illegible]	[illegible]	–	[illegible]	[illegible]	[illegible]	–	[illegible]	[illegible]	[illegible]	[illegible]	[illegible]	Parsonstown.
–	–	[illegible]	[illegible]	–	[illegible]	–	–	–	–	[illegible]	[illegible]	[illegible]	[illegible]	Tullamore.
														Longford:
–	–	[illegible]	–	–	–	–	–	–	[illegible]	[illegible]	[illegible]	[illegible]	[illegible]	Granard.
–	–	[illegible]	–	–	–	–	–	–	–	[illegible]	[illegible]	[illegible]	[illegible]	Longford.
														Louth:
–	[illegible]	[illegible]	[illegible]	–	–	–	–	–	–	[illegible]	[illegible]	[illegible]	[illegible]	Ardee.
–	[illegible]	[illegible]	[illegible]	–	[illegible]	[illegible]	[illegible]	[illegible]	[illegible]	[illegible]	[illegible]	–	[illegible]	Dundalk.
														Meath:
[illegible]	[illegible]	[illegible]	[illegible]	–	[illegible]	[illegible]	[illegible]	–	–	[illegible]	[illegible]	[illegible]	[illegible]	Kells.
–	–	[illegible]	[illegible]	–	–	[illegible]	[illegible]	–	[illegible]	[illegible]	[illegible]	[illegible]	[illegible]	Navan.
–	–	[illegible]	[illegible]	–	[illegible]	[illegible]	–	–	–	[illegible]	[illegible]	–	[illegible]	Trim.
														Queen's:
–	[illegible]	[illegible]	–	–	–	–	–	–	[illegible]	[illegible]	[illegible]	[illegible]	[illegible]	Maryborough.
–	[illegible]	[illegible]	–	–	–	–	–	–	–	[illegible]	[illegible]	[illegible]	[illegible]	Mountmellick.
														Westmeath:
–	[illegible]	[illegible]	–	–	[illegible]	[illegible]	[illegible]	–	[illegible]	[illegible]	[illegible]	–	[illegible]	Athlone (pt. in Roscommon).
–	[illegible]	[illegible]	–	–	–	–	–	–	[illegible]	[illegible]	[illegible]	[illegible]	[illegible]	Mullingar.
														Wexford:
–	–	[illegible]	[illegible]	–	[illegible]	[illegible]	[illegible]	–	[illegible]	[illegible]	[illegible]	[illegible]	[illegible]	Enniscorthy.
–	[illegible]	[illegible]	–	–	–	–	–	–	–	[illegible]	[illegible]	[illegible]	[illegible]	Gorey.
[illegible]	[illegible]	[illegible]	[illegible]	–	[illegible]	[illegible]	[illegible]	–	[illegible]	[illegible]	[illegible]	[illegible]	[illegible]	New Ross (pt. in Kilkenny).
														Wicklow:
–	[illegible]	[illegible]	–	–	–	–	–	–	[illegible]	[illegible]	[illegible]	[illegible]	[illegible]	Arklow.
[illegible]	[illegible]	[illegible]	[illegible]	–	[illegible]	[illegible]	[illegible]	[illegible]	[illegible]	[illegible]	[illegible]	[illegible]	[illegible]	Total in Leinster ([illegible]).
														MUNSTER.
														Clare:
–	–	[illegible]	[illegible]	–	[illegible]	–	[illegible]	–	[illegible]	[illegible]	[illegible]	[illegible]	[illegible]	Ennis.
–	–	[illegible]	[illegible]	–	–	[illegible]	[illegible]	–	–	[illegible]	[illegible]	–	[illegible]	Kilrush.
														Cork:
–	–	[illegible]	–	–	[illegible]	–	[illegible]	–	[illegible]	[illegible]	[illegible]	[illegible]	[illegible]	Clonakilty.
–	[illegible]	[illegible]	[illegible]	[illegible]	[illegible]	[illegible]	[illegible]	[illegible]	[illegible]	[illegible]	[illegible]	[illegible]	[illegible]	Fermoy.
[illegible]	–	[illegible]	[illegible]	–	[illegible]	–	[illegible]	–	[illegible]	[illegible]	[illegible]	[illegible]	[illegible]	Kinsale.
–	–	[illegible]	[illegible]	[illegible]	–	–	–	–	[illegible]	[illegible]	[illegible]	[illegible]	[illegible]	Mallow.
–	–	[illegible]	[illegible]	–	–	–	–	–	–	[illegible]	[illegible]	[illegible]	[illegible]	Midleton.
–	[illegible]	[illegible]	[illegible]	[illegible]	[illegible]	[illegible]	[illegible]	–	[illegible]	[illegible]	[illegible]	[illegible]	[illegible]	Queenstown.
–	–	[illegible]	–	[illegible]	–	–	–	–	–	[illegible]	[illegible]	[illegible]	[illegible]	Skibbereen.
														Kerry:
–	–	[illegible]	[illegible]	–	[illegible]	[illegible]	[illegible]	–	[illegible]	[illegible]	[illegible]	–	[illegible]	Killarney.
–	–	[illegible]	–	–	[illegible]	–	–	–	[illegible]	[illegible]	[illegible]	–	[illegible]	Listowel.
–	[illegible]	[illegible]	[illegible]	–	[illegible]	–	[illegible]	[illegible]	[illegible]	[illegible]	[illegible]	–	[illegible]	Tralee.
														Limerick:
–	–	[illegible]	–	–	–	–	–	–	–	[illegible]	[illegible]	[illegible]	[illegible]	Rathkeale.
														Tipperary:
[illegible]	[illegible]	[illegible]	–	–	[illegible]	–	[illegible]	–	[illegible]	[illegible]	[illegible]	[illegible]	[illegible]	Carrick-on-Suir.
[illegible]	–	[illegible]	[illegible]	–	–	–	–	–	[illegible]	[illegible]	[illegible]	[illegible]	[illegible]	Cashel.
–	[illegible]	[illegible]	–	–	–	–	–	–	[illegible]	[illegible]	[illegible]	[illegible]	[illegible]	Nenagh.
–	[illegible]	[illegible]	[illegible]	–	[illegible]	[illegible]	[illegible]	–	[illegible]	[illegible]	[illegible]	[illegible]	[illegible]	Templemore.
–	[illegible]	[illegible]	[illegible]	–	[illegible]	[illegible]	–	–	[illegible]	[illegible]	[illegible]	[illegible]	[illegible]	Thurles.
–	[illegible]	[illegible]	[illegible]	[illegible]	–	–	–	–	–	[illegible]	[illegible]	[illegible]	[illegible]	Tipperary.
														Waterford:
[illegible]	[illegible]	[illegible]	[illegible]	–	[illegible]	[illegible]	[illegible]	–	[illegible]	[illegible]	[illegible]	–	[illegible]	Dungarvan.
–	–	[illegible]	[illegible]	–	–	–	–	–	–	[illegible]	[illegible]	[illegible]	[illegible]	Lismore.
[illegible]	[illegible]	[illegible]	[illegible]	[illegible]	[illegible]	[illegible]	[illegible]	[illegible]	[illegible]	[illegible]	[illegible]	[illegible]	[illegible]	Total in Munster ([illegible]).

V. (continued).—Summary of Returns of Receipts and Expenditure of Town Commissioners under

Towns, arranged in Counties and Provinces.	[illegible]	Receipts. [illegible]	[illegible]	[illegible]	[illegible]	[illegible]	[illegible]	[illegible]	[illegible]	Other Receipts.	Total Receipts.	[illegible]	Total.	[illegible]
Ulster.	£	£	£	£	£	£	£	£	£	£	£	£	£	£
Antrim:														
Antrim,	[illegible]	97	–	–	–	–	–	–	–	16	191	7	111	–
Ballymena,	71[illegible]	[illegible]	–	4,0[illegible]	–	9	–	16	11[illegible]	[illegible]	4,[illegible]	–	6,4[illegible]	–
Ballymoney,	4	[illegible]	–	–	–	40	–	–	4	78	[illegible]	–	1[illegible]	–
Larne,	[illegible]	570	–	640	–	–	–	–	–	1[illegible]	1,[illegible]	–	1,[illegible]	–
Lisburn,	310	2,[illegible]	–	[illegible]	711	45	17,[illegible]	[illegible]	71	445	22,[illegible]	–	22,[illegible]	–
Portrush,	[illegible]	[illegible]	–	–	–	–	–	–	–	[illegible]	[illegible]	–	[illegible]	–
Armagh:														
Keady,	[illegible]	73	–	–	[illegible]	16	–	–	–	44	179	–	[illegible]	–
†Lurgan,	1[illegible]	4,[illegible]	–	2,[illegible]	[illegible]	412	2,[illegible]	–	[illegible]	[illegible]	[illegible]	[illegible]	[illegible]	–
Portadown,	–	1,[illegible]	–	–	775	[illegible]	–	1,[illegible]	15	[illegible]	2,41[illegible]	[illegible]	2,[illegible]	[illegible]
Tandragee,	14	[illegible]	–	–	–	–	–	–	3	4	157	–	141	–
Cavan:														
Belturbet,	347	–	–	–	163	10[illegible]	–	–	–	81	[illegible]	–	[illegible]	–
Cavan,	[illegible]	[illegible]	–	–	–	111	–	–	–	31	[illegible]	[illegible]	[illegible]	–
Cootehill,	17	115	–	–	–	–	–	–	–	17	1[illegible]	–	1[illegible]	–
Donegal:														
Ballyshannon,	[illegible]	[illegible]	–	–	–	–	–	–	–	73	176	–	[illegible]	–
Letterkenny,	[illegible]	[illegible]	–	–	–	–	–	–	8	[illegible]	270	–	[illegible]	–
Down:														
Banbridge,	60	[illegible]	–	–	[illegible]	8	–	–	81	[illegible]	1,[illegible]	[illegible]	1,[illegible]	[illegible]
Bangor,	–	2,211	–	[illegible]	–	[illegible]	4,[illegible]	–	[illegible]	41	6,[illegible]	–	6,[illegible]	[illegible]
Downpatrick,	–	[illegible]	–	–	–	1	–	–	–	44	[illegible]	–	[illegible]	11
Dromore,	[illegible]	773	–	–	[illegible]	[illegible]	–	–	1	[illegible]	347	–	[illegible]	–
Gilford,	[illegible]	[illegible]	–	–	–	–	–	–	–	10	[illegible]	–	[illegible]	–
Holywood,	[illegible]	[illegible]	–	811	–	[illegible]	–	[illegible]	13	[illegible]	1,[illegible]	–	1,[illegible]	–
Newtownards,	–	[illegible]	–	–	873	–	[illegible]	[illegible]	[illegible]	[illegible]	1,[illegible]	[illegible]	2,[illegible]	[illegible]
Warrenpoint,	[illegible]	[illegible]	–	[illegible]	11	[illegible]	–	–	0	[illegible]	[illegible]	–	[illegible]	–
Londonderry:														
Coleraine,	[illegible]	1,[illegible]	–	–	[illegible]	[illegible]	[illegible]	–	[illegible]	[illegible]	4,[illegible]	–	4,[illegible]	–
Limavady,	9	73	–	–	–	–	–	–	–	[illegible]	[illegible]	–	[illegible]	–
Monaghan:														
Ballybay,	[illegible]	[illegible]	–	–	9	–	–	–	–	[illegible]	[illegible]	–	[illegible]	–
Carrickmacross,	[illegible]	[illegible]	–	–	–	–	–	–	–	[illegible]	97	–	110	–
Castleblayney,	[illegible]	[illegible]	–	–	–	–	–	–	–	[illegible]	[illegible]	–	[illegible]	–
Clones,	1[illegible]	1[illegible]	–	–	[illegible]	[illegible]	[illegible]	–	[illegible]	[illegible]	[illegible]	–	[illegible]	–
Tyrone:														
Aughnacloy,	[illegible]	[illegible]	–	–	[illegible]	–	–	–	–	7	41	–	[illegible]	–
Cookstown,	[illegible]	1[illegible]	–	–	–	–	–	–	–	[illegible]	[illegible]	17	[illegible]	–
Strabane,	1[illegible]	[illegible]	–	–	[illegible]	[illegible]	–	–	–	[illegible]	1,[illegible]	–	1,[illegible]	–
Total in Ulster ([illegible]),	4,[illegible]	[illegible]	–	[illegible]	[illegible]	[illegible]	[illegible]	[illegible]	[illegible]	4,[illegible]	[illegible]	[illegible]	[illegible]	[illegible]
Connaught.														
Galway:														
Ballinasloe,	–	[illegible]	[illegible]	–	–	–	–	–	10	[illegible]	701	[illegible]	[illegible]	[illegible]
Loughrea,	1[illegible]	[illegible]	–	–	–	–	–	1[illegible]	–	[illegible]	[illegible]	–	[illegible]	–
Tuam,	–	–	–	–	[illegible]	1	–	–	–	[illegible]	[illegible]	[illegible]	[illegible]	[illegible]
Mayo:														
Ballina,	[illegible]	[illegible]	–	–	–	10	–	–	–	[illegible]	[illegible]	–	2[illegible]	–
Castlebar,	–	11[illegible]	–	–	–	–	–	–	–	[illegible]	[illegible]	–	1[illegible]	[illegible]
Westport,	–	[illegible]	–	–	–	–	–	–	–	[illegible]	[illegible]	–	[illegible]	–
Roscommon:														
Boyle,	–	[illegible]	–	–	–	5	–	–	–	37	1[illegible]	–	1[illegible]	3
Roscommon,	–	[illegible]	–	–	[illegible]	[illegible]	–	–	–	[illegible]	[illegible]	–	[illegible]	[illegible]
Total in Connaught ([illegible]),	1[illegible]	1,[illegible]	[illegible]	–	[illegible]	67	–	1[illegible]	[illegible]	[illegible]	[illegible]	[illegible]	[illegible]	[illegible]
Total in Ireland ([illegible]) 1863,	[illegible]	[illegible]	[illegible]	[illegible]	7,[illegible]	[illegible]	[illegible]	[illegible]	[illegible]	[illegible]	[illegible]	[illegible]	[illegible]	[illegible]
Total in Ireland ([illegible]) 1864,	[illegible]	[illegible]	[illegible]	[illegible]	[illegible]	[illegible]	[illegible]	[illegible]	[illegible]	[illegible]	[illegible]	[illegible]	[illegible]	[illegible]
Increase,	[illegible]	[illegible]	[illegible]	[illegible]	[illegible]	[illegible]	[illegible]	–	[illegible]	[illegible]	[illegible]	[illegible]	[illegible]	[illegible]
Decrease,	–	–	–	–	–	–	–	[illegible]	–	–	–	–	–	–

*See notes, page [illegible]. † The amounts in this case are for a year and a half, but [illegible]

Towns Improvement (Ireland) Act, 1854 (17 & 18 Vic., c. 103), for the financial year ended in 1895.

Expenditure														
[illegible]	[illegible]	[illegible]	[illegible]	[illegible]	Water supply.	[illegible]	Other sanitary purposes.	[illegible]	[illegible]	[illegible]	[illegible]	[illegible]	Total.	Towns, arranged in Provinces and Counties.
£	£	£	£	£	£	£	£	£	£	£	£	£	£	Ulster.
														Antrim:
[illegible]	[illegible]	[illegible]	[illegible]	[illegible]	[illegible]	[illegible]	[illegible]	[illegible]	[illegible]	[illegible]	[illegible]	[illegible]	[illegible]	Antrim.
[illegible]	[illegible]	[illegible]	[illegible]	[illegible]	[illegible]	[illegible]	[illegible]	[illegible]	[illegible]	[illegible]	[illegible]	[illegible]	[illegible]	Ballymena.
[illegible]	[illegible]	[illegible]	[illegible]	[illegible]	[illegible]	[illegible]	[illegible]	[illegible]	[illegible]	[illegible]	[illegible]	[illegible]	[illegible]	Ballymoney.
[illegible]	[illegible]	[illegible]	[illegible]	[illegible]	[illegible]	[illegible]	[illegible]	[illegible]	[illegible]	[illegible]	[illegible]	[illegible]	[illegible]	Larne.
[illegible]	[illegible]	[illegible]	[illegible]	[illegible]	[illegible]	[illegible]	[illegible]	[illegible]	[illegible]	[illegible]	[illegible]	[illegible]	[illegible]	Lisburn.
[illegible]	[illegible]	[illegible]	[illegible]	[illegible]	[illegible]	[illegible]	[illegible]	[illegible]	[illegible]	[illegible]	[illegible]	[illegible]	[illegible]	Portrush.
														Armagh:
[illegible]	[illegible]	[illegible]	[illegible]	[illegible]	[illegible]	[illegible]	[illegible]	[illegible]	[illegible]	[illegible]	[illegible]	[illegible]	[illegible]	Keady.
[illegible]	[illegible]	[illegible]	[illegible]	[illegible]	[illegible]	[illegible]	[illegible]	[illegible]	[illegible]	[illegible]	[illegible]	[illegible]	[illegible]	Lurgan.
[illegible]	[illegible]	[illegible]	[illegible]	[illegible]	[illegible]	[illegible]	[illegible]	[illegible]	[illegible]	[illegible]	[illegible]	[illegible]	[illegible]	Portadown.
[illegible]	[illegible]	[illegible]	[illegible]	[illegible]	[illegible]	[illegible]	[illegible]	[illegible]	[illegible]	[illegible]	[illegible]	[illegible]	[illegible]	Tandragee.
														Cavan:
[illegible]	[illegible]	[illegible]	[illegible]	[illegible]	[illegible]	[illegible]	[illegible]	[illegible]	[illegible]	[illegible]	[illegible]	[illegible]	[illegible]	Belturbet.
[illegible]	[illegible]	[illegible]	[illegible]	[illegible]	[illegible]	[illegible]	[illegible]	[illegible]	[illegible]	[illegible]	[illegible]	[illegible]	[illegible]	Cavan.
[illegible]	[illegible]	[illegible]	[illegible]	[illegible]	[illegible]	[illegible]	[illegible]	[illegible]	[illegible]	[illegible]	[illegible]	[illegible]	[illegible]	Cootehill.
														Donegal:
[illegible]	[illegible]	[illegible]	[illegible]	[illegible]	[illegible]	[illegible]	[illegible]	[illegible]	[illegible]	[illegible]	[illegible]	[illegible]	[illegible]	Ballyshannon.
[illegible]	[illegible]	[illegible]	[illegible]	[illegible]	[illegible]	[illegible]	[illegible]	[illegible]	[illegible]	[illegible]	[illegible]	[illegible]	[illegible]	Letterkenny.
														Down:
[illegible]	[illegible]	[illegible]	[illegible]	[illegible]	[illegible]	[illegible]	[illegible]	[illegible]	[illegible]	[illegible]	[illegible]	[illegible]	[illegible]	Banbridge.
[illegible]	[illegible]	[illegible]	[illegible]	[illegible]	[illegible]	[illegible]	[illegible]	[illegible]	[illegible]	[illegible]	[illegible]	[illegible]	[illegible]	Bangor.
[illegible]	[illegible]	[illegible]	[illegible]	[illegible]	[illegible]	[illegible]	[illegible]	[illegible]	[illegible]	[illegible]	[illegible]	[illegible]	[illegible]	Downpatrick.
[illegible]	[illegible]	[illegible]	[illegible]	[illegible]	[illegible]	[illegible]	[illegible]	[illegible]	[illegible]	[illegible]	[illegible]	[illegible]	[illegible]	Dromore.
[illegible]	[illegible]	[illegible]	[illegible]	[illegible]	[illegible]	[illegible]	[illegible]	[illegible]	[illegible]	[illegible]	[illegible]	[illegible]	[illegible]	Gilford.
[illegible]	[illegible]	[illegible]	[illegible]	[illegible]	[illegible]	[illegible]	[illegible]	[illegible]	[illegible]	[illegible]	[illegible]	[illegible]	[illegible]	Holywood.
[illegible]	[illegible]	[illegible]	[illegible]	[illegible]	[illegible]	[illegible]	[illegible]	[illegible]	[illegible]	[illegible]	[illegible]	[illegible]	[illegible]	Newtownards.
[illegible]	[illegible]	[illegible]	[illegible]	[illegible]	[illegible]	[illegible]	[illegible]	[illegible]	[illegible]	[illegible]	[illegible]	[illegible]	[illegible]	Warrenpoint.
														Londonderry:
[illegible]	[illegible]	[illegible]	[illegible]	[illegible]	[illegible]	[illegible]	[illegible]	[illegible]	[illegible]	[illegible]	[illegible]	[illegible]	[illegible]	Coleraine.
[illegible]	[illegible]	[illegible]	[illegible]	[illegible]	[illegible]	[illegible]	[illegible]	[illegible]	[illegible]	[illegible]	[illegible]	[illegible]	[illegible]	Limavady.
														Monaghan:
[illegible]	[illegible]	[illegible]	[illegible]	[illegible]	[illegible]	[illegible]	[illegible]	[illegible]	[illegible]	[illegible]	[illegible]	[illegible]	[illegible]	Ballybay.
[illegible]	[illegible]	[illegible]	[illegible]	[illegible]	[illegible]	[illegible]	[illegible]	[illegible]	[illegible]	[illegible]	[illegible]	[illegible]	[illegible]	Carrickmacross.
[illegible]	[illegible]	[illegible]	[illegible]	[illegible]	[illegible]	[illegible]	[illegible]	[illegible]	[illegible]	[illegible]	[illegible]	[illegible]	[illegible]	Castleblayney.
[illegible]	[illegible]	[illegible]	[illegible]	[illegible]	[illegible]	[illegible]	[illegible]	[illegible]	[illegible]	[illegible]	[illegible]	[illegible]	[illegible]	Clones.
														Tyrone:
[illegible]	[illegible]	[illegible]	[illegible]	[illegible]	[illegible]	[illegible]	[illegible]	[illegible]	[illegible]	[illegible]	[illegible]	[illegible]	[illegible]	Aughnacloy.
[illegible]	[illegible]	[illegible]	[illegible]	[illegible]	[illegible]	[illegible]	[illegible]	[illegible]	[illegible]	[illegible]	[illegible]	[illegible]	[illegible]	Cookstown.
[illegible]	[illegible]	[illegible]	[illegible]	[illegible]	[illegible]	[illegible]	[illegible]	[illegible]	[illegible]	[illegible]	[illegible]	[illegible]	[illegible]	Strabane.
[illegible]	[illegible]	[illegible]	[illegible]	-	[illegible]	[illegible]	[illegible]	[illegible]	[illegible]	[illegible]	[illegible]	[illegible]	[illegible]	Total in Ulster (31).
														Connaught.
														Galway:
[illegible]	[illegible]	[illegible]	[illegible]	[illegible]	[illegible]	[illegible]	[illegible]	[illegible]	[illegible]	[illegible]	[illegible]	[illegible]	[illegible]	Ballinasloe.
[illegible]	[illegible]	[illegible]	[illegible]	[illegible]	[illegible]	[illegible]	[illegible]	[illegible]	[illegible]	[illegible]	[illegible]	[illegible]	[illegible]	Loughrea.
[illegible]	[illegible]	[illegible]	[illegible]	[illegible]	[illegible]	[illegible]	[illegible]	[illegible]	[illegible]	[illegible]	[illegible]	[illegible]	[illegible]	Tuam.
														Mayo:
[illegible]	[illegible]	[illegible]	[illegible]	[illegible]	[illegible]	[illegible]	[illegible]	[illegible]	[illegible]	[illegible]	[illegible]	[illegible]	[illegible]	Ballina.
[illegible]	[illegible]	[illegible]	[illegible]	[illegible]	[illegible]	[illegible]	[illegible]	[illegible]	[illegible]	[illegible]	[illegible]	[illegible]	[illegible]	Castlebar.
[illegible]	[illegible]	[illegible]	[illegible]	[illegible]	[illegible]	[illegible]	[illegible]	[illegible]	[illegible]	[illegible]	[illegible]	[illegible]	[illegible]	Westport.
														Roscommon:
[illegible]	[illegible]	[illegible]	[illegible]	[illegible]	[illegible]	[illegible]	[illegible]	[illegible]	[illegible]	[illegible]	[illegible]	[illegible]	[illegible]	Boyle.
[illegible]	[illegible]	[illegible]	[illegible]	[illegible]	[illegible]	[illegible]	[illegible]	[illegible]	[illegible]	[illegible]	[illegible]	[illegible]	[illegible]	Roscommon.
[illegible]	[illegible]	[illegible]	[illegible]	-	[illegible]	-	[illegible]	-	[illegible]	[illegible]	[illegible]	[illegible]	[illegible]	Total in Connaught (8).
[illegible]	[illegible]	[illegible]	[illegible]	[illegible]	[illegible]	[illegible]	[illegible]	[illegible]	[illegible]	[illegible]	[illegible]	[illegible]	[illegible]	1895. Total in Ireland (80)*
[illegible]	[illegible]	[illegible]	[illegible]	[illegible]	[illegible]	[illegible]	[illegible]	[illegible]	[illegible]	[illegible]	[illegible]	[illegible]	[illegible]	1894. Total in Ireland
[illegible]	[illegible]	-	[illegible]	[illegible]	[illegible]	[illegible]	[illegible]	[illegible]	[illegible]	[illegible]	[illegible]	-	[illegible]	Increase.
-	-	[illegible]	-	-	-	-	-	-	-	-	-	[illegible]	-	Decrease.

[illegible]

VI.—Lighting and Cleansing Commissioners (Act 9 Geo. IV., cap. 82). Summary of the

[illegible]	[illegible]	Receipts.										[illegible]	Total.
		9 Geo. IV. c. 82.	[illegible]	[illegible]	[illegible]	[illegible]	[illegible]	[illegible]	[illegible]	[illegible]	[illegible]		
Leinster.	£	£	£	£	£	£	£	£	£	£	£	£	£
Wicklow:													
Wicklow, . .	350	–	–	431	10	-	-	0	1,[illegible]	250	1,[illegible]	-	[illegible]
Munster.													
Cork:													
Bandon, . .	200	[illegible]	-	-	-	-	-	–	-	34	235	-	[illegible]
*Youghal, . .	-	[illegible]	-	282	0	1,[illegible]	70	17	482	644	7,191	-	7,[illegible]
Tipperary:													
Fethard, . .	14	-	-	-	40	-	-	-	65	14	141	-	177
Ulster.													
Armagh:													
†Armagh, . .	654	734	–	650	–	–	-	18	–	173	1,[illegible]	-	2,[illegible]
Monaghan:													
Monaghan, . .	179	231	–	–	-	–	-	2	4	60	331	–	[illegible]
Tyrone:													
Dungannon, . .	10	524	–	–	-	-	-	-	-	30	555	-	[illegible]
Omagh, . .	65	387	–	-	–	–	–	–	–	113	500	-	[illegible]
Total, 1878,	1,[illegible]	3,[illegible]	-	1,[illegible]	41	3,[illegible]	80	35	1,814	1,179	12,142	-	13,[illegible]
Total, 1868,	1,171	1,646	-	1,320	75	-	-	30	3,[illegible]	2,[illegible]	7,[illegible]	554	9,1[illegible]
Increase, . .	620	10	–	–	-	3,[illegible]	80	-	–	-	4,[illegible]	-	4,[illegible]
Decrease, . .	-	-	–	257	14	–	-	-	225	475	–	554	-

[illegible]

[illegible]

receipts and expenditure of the Commissioners during the financial year ended in 1886.

[illegible] of the past year	Expenditure. Lighting [illegible]	[illegible]	[illegible]	[illegible]	Water supply.	[illegible]	[illegible]	[illegible]	[illegible]	[illegible]	[illegible] of the year	Total.	[illegible]
£	£	£	£	£	£	£	£	£	£	£	£	£	LEINSTER.
													Wicklow:
–	[illegible]	97	[illegible]	–	–	–	–	911	[illegible]	[illegible]	[illegible]	[illegible]	Wicklow.
													MUNSTER.
													Cork:
–	[illegible]	–	–	[illegible]	–	–	–	[illegible]	[illegible]	[illegible]	18	[illegible]	Bandon.
[illegible]	[illegible]	116	[illegible]	–	[illegible]	9	[illegible]	[illegible]	[illegible]	[illegible]	[illegible]	7,161	Youghal.
													Tipperary:
–	[illegible]	–	9	–	–	–	–	–	117	371	8	117	Fethard.
													ULSTER.
													Armagh:
–	[illegible]	[illegible]	[illegible]	[illegible]	[illegible]	[illegible]	[illegible]	[illegible]	[illegible]	[illegible]	[illegible]	[illegible]	Armagh.
													Monaghan:
–	[illegible]	[illegible]	–	[illegible]	[illegible]	–	–	–	[illegible]	[illegible]	[illegible]	[illegible]	Monaghan.
													Tyrone:
–	[illegible]	–	–	–	–	–	–	–	[illegible]	[illegible]	[illegible]	[illegible]	Dungannon.
–	[illegible]	–	[illegible]	[illegible]	–	–	–	–	[illegible]	[illegible]	77	[illegible]	Omagh.
[illegible]	[illegible]	[illegible]	[illegible]	[illegible]	[illegible]	97	140	[illegible]	[illegible]	[illegible]	[illegible]	[illegible]	[illegible] } Total.
[illegible]	[illegible]	[illegible]	[illegible]	[illegible]	[illegible]	[illegible]	[illegible]	[illegible]	[illegible]	[illegible]	[illegible]	9,711	[illegible] } Total.
–	–	41	[illegible]	5	[illegible]	4	–	[illegible]	[illegible]	[illegible]	[illegible]	[illegible]	Increase.
[illegible]	[illegible]	–	–	–	–	–	57	–	–	–	–	–	Decrease.

VII.—Commissioners under Special Acts. Summary of returns of sums received by Commissioners, [illegible] Commissioners under 3 and 4 Vic., c. 108, section 16,

Part I.—Receipts

Towns and other Townships, arranged in Provinces (11 Towns and Townships).	Statutes under which constituted.	Balance in favour of the Commissioners at the beginning of the year.	Revenue.		
			Rates ...	Other Rate.	Fines, Market, Fees, &c.
1.	2.	3.	4.	5.	6.
LEINSTER.		£	£	£	£
Dublin City:					
Fitzwilliam-square (Commissioners),	[illegible] Geo. III., c. [illegible]	No	return.	-	-
Merrion-square (Commissioners),	[illegible] Geo. III., c. [illegible] (Ir.); and [illegible] Geo. III., c. [illegible] (Ir.) s. [illegible]	No	return.	-	-
Mountjoy-square (Commissioners),	[illegible] Geo. III., c. [illegible]	No	return.	-	-
Rutland-square (Governors of Lying-in Hospital),	[illegible] Geo. III., c. [illegible] (Ir.).	-	-	[illegible]	-
Dublin County:					
Blackrock Township (Commissioners),	[illegible] & [illegible] Vic., c. [illegible]	-	[illegible]	[illegible]	-
Clontarf Ditto,	[illegible] & [illegible] Vic., c. [illegible]	[illegible]	[illegible]	[illegible]	-
Dalkey Ditto,	[illegible] & [illegible] Vic., c. [illegible]	[illegible]	[illegible]	-	-
Drumcondra, Clonliffe, and Glasnevin Township (Commissioners).	[illegible] & [illegible] Vic., c. [illegible]	-	[illegible]	-	-
Kilmainham (New) Ditto,	[illegible] & [illegible] Vic., c. [illegible]	-	[illegible]	-	-
Kingstown Ditto,	[illegible] & [illegible] Vic., c. [illegible], and other Acts	[illegible]	[illegible]	[illegible]	[illegible]
Pembroke Ditto,	[illegible] & [illegible] Vic., c. [illegible], and other Acts.	-	[illegible]	-	-
Rathmines and Rathgar Township (Improvement Commissioners).	10 & 11 Vic., c. [illegible], and other Acts	[illegible]	[illegible]	-	-
Wicklow County and Dublin County:					
Bray Township (Commissioners),	[illegible] & [illegible] Vic., c. [illegible]; and [illegible] & [illegible] Vic., c. [illegible]	[illegible]	[illegible]	[illegible]	[illegible]
ULSTER.					
Belfast City and District, Water Commissioners,	[illegible] & [illegible] Vic., c. [illegible]; [illegible] & [illegible] Vic., c. [illegible], and other Acts.	[illegible]	-	[illegible]	-
Carrickfergus (Municipal Commissioners),	[illegible] & [illegible] Vic., c. [illegible]; [illegible] & [illegible] Vic., c. [illegible]; and [illegible] & [illegible] Vic., [illegible]	[illegible]	-	-	[illegible]
[illegible] (Commissioners of the Borough),	[illegible] & [illegible] Vic., c. [illegible]	[illegible]	[illegible]	[illegible]	-
Newry (Commissioners),	[illegible] & [illegible] Vic., c. [illegible]	-	[illegible]	[illegible]	[illegible]
CONNAUGHT.					
Galway Town (Improvement Commissioners),	[illegible] & [illegible] Vic., c. [illegible]	[illegible]	[illegible]	[illegible]	[illegible]
	Total for 11 Towns and Townships,	[illegible]	[illegible]	[illegible]	[illegible]
	Grand total, [illegible]	[illegible]	[illegible]	[illegible]	[illegible]
	Grand total, [illegible]	[illegible]	[illegible]	[illegible]	[illegible]
	Increase,	—	—	[illegible]	—
	Decrease,	[illegible]	[illegible]	—	[illegible]

having powers of local taxation under special Acts, and in one case (Carrickfergus) by Municipal for the financial year ended in 1883.

during financial year.

Receipts. [illegible] 1.	[illegible]	[illegible]	[illegible]	Other receipts.	Total receipts.	Balance in hand at the close of the year.	Total.	Towns and other Districts, etc.
£	£	£	£	£	£	£	£	LEINSTER.
								Dublin City:
-	-	-	-	-	-	-	-	Fitzwilliam-square (Commissioners).
-	-	-	-	-	-	-	-	[illegible]-square (Commissioners).
-	-	-	-	-	-	-	-	Mountjoy-square (Commissioners).
	-	-	-	-	191	-	[illegible]	Rutland-square (Governors of Lying-in Hospital).
								Dublin County:
97	1,4[illegible]	[illegible]	217	[illegible]	10,[illegible]	671	14,[illegible]	Blackrock Township (Commissioners).
64	[illegible]	-	[illegible]	[illegible]	[illegible]	-	[illegible]	Clontarf Ditto.
67	-	-	81	[illegible]	[illegible]	-	[illegible]	Dalkey Ditto.
-	-	-	[illegible]	[illegible]	[illegible]	-	[illegible]	Drumcondra, Clonliffe, and Glasnevin Township (Commissioners).
-	[illegible]	-	[illegible]	[illegible]	2,519	164	[illegible]	Kilmainham (New) Ditto.
[illegible]	[illegible]	[illegible]	[illegible]	[illegible]	37,[illegible]	[illegible]	[illegible]	Kingstown Ditto.
[illegible]	[illegible]	-	[illegible]	[illegible]	[illegible]	[illegible]	[illegible]	Pembroke Ditto.
176	[illegible]	-	[illegible]	[illegible]	[illegible]	-	[illegible]	Rathmines and Rathgar Township (Improvement Commissioners).
								Wicklow County and Dublin County:
[illegible]	[illegible]	-	[illegible]	[illegible]	[illegible]	-	[illegible]	Bray Township (Commissioners).
								ULSTER.
-	[illegible]	[illegible]	-	[illegible]	[illegible]	-	[illegible]	Belfast City and District, Water Commissioners.
[illegible]	-	-	[illegible]	[illegible]	[illegible]	-	[illegible]	Carrickfergus (Municipal Commissioners).
[illegible]	[illegible]	-	[illegible]	[illegible]	[illegible]	[illegible]	[illegible]	Enniskillen (Commissioners of the Borough).
[illegible]	[illegible]	-	[illegible]	[illegible]	[illegible]	-	[illegible]	Newry (Commissioners).
								CONNAUGHT.
[illegible]	-	-	[illegible]	[illegible]	[illegible]	-	[illegible]	Galway Town (Improvement Commissioners).
[illegible]	[illegible]	[illegible]	[illegible]	[illegible]	[illegible]	[illegible]	[illegible]	Total for 15 Towns and Townships.
[illegible]	[illegible]	[illegible]	[illegible]	[illegible]	[illegible]	[illegible]	[illegible]	[illegible] } Grand total.
[illegible]	[illegible]	[illegible]	[illegible]	[illegible]	[illegible]	[illegible]	[illegible]	[illegible] }
-	[illegible]	-	[illegible]	-	[illegible]	-	[illegible]	Increase.
[illegible]	-	[illegible]	-	[illegible]	-	[illegible]	-	Decrease.

VII. (continued.)—COMMISSIONERS UNDER SPECIAL ACTS. SUMMARY of returns of expenditure by Municipal Commissioners under 3 and 4 Vic., c. 108,

PART II.—Expenditure

[illegible]	[illegible]	[illegible]	[illegible]				
			[illegible]	[illegible]	[illegible]	[illegible]	Watching.
1.	2.	3.	4.	5.	6.	7.	8.
LEINSTER.		£	£	£	£	£	£
Dublin City:							
Fitzwilliam-square (Commrs.),	49 Geo. III., c. 163.	No return.		-	-	-	-
Merrion-square (Commrs.),	41 Geo. III., c. 45 (Ir.), and 46 Geo. III., c. 62 (Ir.), c. 11.	No return.		-	-	-	-
Mountjoy-square (Commissrs.),	49 Geo. III., c. 84.	No return.		-	-	-	-
Rutland-square (Governors of Lying-in Hospital).	25 Geo. III., c. 43 (Ir.)	-	-	-	-	181	-
Dublin County:							
Blackrock Township (Commrs.),	23 & 27 Vic., c. cxx.	413	-	1,280	1,050	480	-
Clontarf Ditto,	32 & 33 Vic., c. lxxx.	-	-	1,109	697	402	-
Dalkey Ditto,	30 & 31 Vic., c. cxxvi.	-	-	376	35	450	-
Drumcondra, Clonliffe, and Glasnevin Township (Commrs.)	41 & 42 Vic., c. clvi.	678	-	1,322	-	301	-
Kilmainham (New) Ditto,	32 & 33 Vic., c. cx.	301	-	620	-	64	-
Kingstown Ditto,	24 & 25 Vic., c. cxiii, and other Acts.	-	-	1,944	807	1,471	-
Pembroke Ditto,	26 & 27 Vic., c. lxxii, and other Acts.	6,[illegible]	1,049	4,843	-	1,095	-
Rathmines and Rathgar Township (Improvement Commrs.)	10 & 11 Vic., c. ccliii, and other Acts.	-	7,810	6,164	-	1,000	-
Wicklow County and Dublin County:							
Bray Township (Commissioners),	29 & 30 Vic., c. cclxi; and 33 & 34 Vic., c. xcii.	-	2,444	453	380	600	-
ULSTER.							
Belfast City and District, Water Commissioners.	23 & 24 Vic., c. clxxxiv; 41 & 42 Vic., c. civ; and other Acts.	-	-	-	-	-	-
Carrickfergus (Municipal Commissioners).	5 & 6 Vic., c. 103; 6 & 7 Vic., c. 93; and 28 & 29 Vic., cap. lxxi.	-	-	-	20	104	-
Enniskillen (Commissioners of the Borough).	23 & 24 Vic., c. cxlii.	-	771	438	371	381	-
Newry (Commissioners),	24 & 25 Vic., c. cxviii.	1,276	-	667	673	285	-
CONNAUGHT.							
Galway Town (Improvement Commrs.)	15 & 16 Vic., c. cx.	-	-	940	1,030	648	187
	Total for 13 Towns and Townships,	7,[illegible]	11,074	20,730	4,643	6,880	187
	Grand total, 1883	7,[illegible]	11,296	20,737	4,644	6,863	187
	Grand total, 1884	7,[illegible]	14,[illegible]	19,020	7,278	6,861	190
	Increase,	-	-	1,716	-	102	-
	Decrease,	343	3,311	-	2,630	-	3

* [illegible] of this [illegible]

Commissioners having powers of local taxation under special Acts, and in one case (Carrickfergus) by section 16, for the financial year ended in 1895.

during financial year.

Expenditure: Water supply.	Expenditure: [illegible]	Expenditure: Other sanitary [illegible]	Contributions to County expenditure.	Payments in respect of borrowed money.	Other expenses.	Total expenditure.	Balance at end of year.	Total.	Towns and other districts (names of Commissioners.)
9.	10.	11.	12.	13.	14.	15.	16.	17.	18.
£	£	£	£	£	£	£	£	£	LEINSTER.
									Dublin City:
-	-	-	-	-	-	-	-	-	Fitzwilliam-square (Commissioners).
-	-	-	-	-	-	-	-	-	Merrion-square (Commissioners).
-	-	-	-	-	-	-	-	-	Mountjoy-square (Commissioners).
-	-	-	-	-	[illegible]	[illegible]	-	[illegible]	Rutland-square (Governors of Lying-in Hospital).
									Dublin County:
[illegible]	[illegible]	[illegible]	[illegible]	[illegible]	[illegible]	[illegible]	-	[illegible]	Kilmainham Township (Commissioners).
[illegible]	[illegible]	[illegible]	[illegible]	[illegible]	[illegible]	[illegible]	[illegible]	[illegible]	Clontarf Ditto.
[illegible]	[illegible]	[illegible]	[illegible]	[illegible]	[illegible]	[illegible]	[illegible]	[illegible]	Dalkey Ditto.
[illegible]	[illegible]	[illegible]	[illegible]	[illegible]	[illegible]	[illegible]	[illegible]	[illegible]	Drumcondra, Clonliffe, and Glasnevin Township Commissioners.
[illegible]	[illegible]	[illegible]	[illegible]	[illegible]	[illegible]	[illegible]	-	[illegible]	Killiney (New) Ditto.
[illegible]	[illegible]	[illegible]	[illegible]	[illegible]	[illegible]	[illegible]	-	[illegible]	Kingstown Ditto.
[illegible]	[illegible]	[illegible]	[illegible]	[illegible]	[illegible]	[illegible]	-	[illegible]	Pembroke Ditto.
[illegible]	[illegible]	[illegible]	[illegible]	[illegible]	[illegible]	[illegible]	[illegible]	[illegible]	Rathmines and Rathgar Township (Improvement Commissioners).
									Wicklow County and Dublin County:
[illegible]	[illegible]	[illegible]	[illegible]	[illegible]	[illegible]	[illegible]	[illegible]	[illegible]	Bray Township (Commissioners).
									ULSTER.
[illegible]	-	-	-	[illegible]	[illegible]	[illegible]	[illegible]	[illegible]	Belfast City and District, Water Commissioners.
[illegible]	[illegible]	[illegible]	-	[illegible]	[illegible]	[illegible]	[illegible]	[illegible]	Carrickfergus (Municipal Commissioners).
[illegible]	[illegible]	[illegible]	[illegible]	[illegible]	[illegible]	[illegible]	-	[illegible]	Enniskillen (Commissioners of the Borough).
[illegible]	[illegible]	[illegible]	[illegible]	[illegible]	[illegible]	[illegible]	[illegible]	[illegible]	Newry (Commissioners).
									CONNAUGHT.
[illegible]	[illegible]	[illegible]	-	[illegible]	[illegible]	[illegible]	[illegible]	[illegible]	Galway Town (Improvement Commissioners.)
[illegible]	[illegible]	[illegible]	[illegible]	[illegible]	[illegible]	[illegible]	[illegible]	[illegible]	Total for 13 Towns and Townships.
[illegible]	[illegible]	[illegible]	[illegible]	[illegible]	[illegible]	[illegible]	[illegible]	[illegible]	1895 } Grand total.
[illegible]	[illegible]	[illegible]	[illegible]	[illegible]	[illegible]	[illegible]	[illegible]	[illegible]	1894 } Grand total.
-	[illegible]	[illegible]	-	[illegible]	[illegible]	[illegible]	[illegible]	[illegible]	Increase.
[illegible]	-	-	[illegible]	-	-	-	-	-	Decrease.

[illegible] brought to [illegible].

VIII.—SUMMARY of local taxes received by the Dublin Metropolitan Police Commissioner for year ended the 31st of March, 189[illegible].

RECEIPTS.				£ s. d.	DISBURSEMENTS.	£ s. d.
From taxation under Acts:—					Paid into Treasury in aid of cost of Metropolitan police,	[illegible] 7 0
Dublin Metropolitan Police tax,				[illegible] 11 [illegible]		
Carriage duty,	£3,17[illegible]	10	0			
Pawnbrokers' licences,	[illegible]	4	7			
[illegible] and [illegible] certificates,	[illegible]	17	6			
Fees from Police courts,	1,[illegible]	[illegible]	6			
				[illegible] 0 [illegible]		
Fines and Penalties from Police courts,				[illegible] 3 7		
Total from taxation,				[illegible] 15 6		
Incidentals, pay of police specially employed, sale of cast clothing, &c.,				1,[illegible] 7 1		
Total receipts applicable to reduction of expenditure,				[illegible] 7 [illegible]	Total,	£[illegible] 7 [illegible]

IX.—SUMMARY of taxes lodged to the credit of the Port and Docks Board, Dublin.

RECEIPTS.	£ s. d.	£ s. d.	EXPENDITURE.	£ s. d.
Balance,		[illegible] 6 3	Repairs of quay walls and bridges,	[illegible] 17 [illegible]
Quay Wall and Bridge tax,	[illegible] 5 [illegible]		Repayment of loans,	[illegible] 12 0
Bridge rate,	4,[illegible] 4 0		Interest,	1,[illegible] 7 [illegible]
Three local taxes,	[illegible] 1 [illegible]		Maintenance of new bridges,	[illegible]
Other receipts,	[illegible] 15 [illegible]			
		[illegible] 7 [illegible]	Total,	£[illegible] 7 0
			Balance,	[illegible] 3 1
Total,		£[illegible] 10 10	Total,	£[illegible] 10 10

X.—COUNTY LEVY PRESENTMENTS in Manor of Kilulagh, including town of Lisburn.

	£ s. d.
Total amount presented on separate Constabularies,	—
" " on Manor at large,	—
Total presented,	—
Total amount levied,	—

TABLE XI.

RECEIPTS and EXPENDITURE of BURIAL BOARDS

XI.—RECEIPTS and Expenditure of Burial Boards

NOTE.—This table, which has been compiled from returns received from Clerks to Burial Boards, does not

Burial Boards.	Balance in favour of the Board at the beginning of the financial year.	Receipts: From rates	Receipts: Fees and payments for interments	Receipts: Money borrowed on security of rates	Receipts: Other receipts	Receipts: Total brought during the year	[illegible]	Total.	Balance against the Board at the end of the financial year.
RURAL BOARDS.	£ s. d.	£ s. d.	£ s. d.	£ s. d.	£ s. d.	£ s. d.	£ s. d.	£ s. d.	£ s. d.
[illegible]	[illegible]	[illegible]	[illegible]	[illegible]	[illegible]	[illegible]	[illegible]	[illegible]	[illegible]

during the financial year ended in 1893.

[illegible]clude the names of any Board which has been returned as having no receipts or expenditure during the year.

Expenditure.								Total expenditure during the year.	Balance in favour at the close of the financial year.	Loan	Burial Boards.
[illegible]	Repairs and drainage, &c.	Maintenance of old ground.	Building and repairs of chapels, &c.	Payments of instalments.	Salaries and wages other than payments of [illegible]	Interest and principal paid off	Rates, taxes, and other payments.				
£ s. d.	£ s. d.	£ s. d.	£ s. d.	£ s. d.	£ s. d.	£ s. d.	£ s. d.	£ s. d.	£ s. d.	£ s. d.	Local Boards.
[illegible]	[illegible]	[illegible]	[illegible]	[illegible]	[illegible]	[illegible]	[illegible]	[illegible]	[illegible]	[illegible]	[illegible]

XI.—(continued)—Receipts and Expenditure of Burial [illegible]

[illegible]	Balance in hand at the commencement of the financial year.	Receipts: Fees, &c.	[illegible]	[illegible]	Other receipts.	Total receipts during the year.	[illegible]	Total.	[illegible]
	£ s. d.	£ s. d.	£ s. d.	£ s. d.	£ s. d.	£ s. d.	£ s. d.	£ s. d.	£ s. d.
Rural Boards—con.									
[illegible]	[illegible]	[illegible]	[illegible]	[illegible]	[illegible]	[illegible]	[illegible]	[illegible]	[illegible]
Total,	[illegible]	[illegible]	[illegible]	[illegible]	[illegible]	[illegible]	[illegible]	[illegible]	[illegible]
Urban Boards.									
[illegible]	[illegible]	[illegible]	[illegible]	[illegible]	[illegible]	[illegible]	[illegible]	[illegible]	[illegible]
Total,	[illegible]	[illegible]	[illegible]	[illegible]	[illegible]	[illegible]	[illegible]	[illegible]	[illegible]
Joint Rural and Urban Boards.									
[illegible]	[illegible]	[illegible]	[illegible]	[illegible]	[illegible]	[illegible]	[illegible]	[illegible]	[illegible]
Total,	[illegible]	[illegible]	[illegible]	[illegible]	[illegible]	[illegible]	[illegible]	[illegible]	[illegible]
Grand Total,	[illegible]	[illegible]	[illegible]	[illegible]	[illegible]	[illegible]	[illegible]	[illegible]	[illegible]
Increase. Decrease.	[illegible]	[illegible]	[illegible]	[illegible]	[illegible]	[illegible]	[illegible]	[illegible]	[illegible]

[illegible] during the financial year ended in 18[illegible].

[illegible]

XII.—Summary of returns made by Clerks of the Peace, of salaries, emoluments, and fees

Counties, and Counties of Cities and of Towns, &c.	Salary.	[illegible]	[illegible]	[illegible]	[illegible]	[illegible]
	£ s. d.	£ s. d.	£ s. d.	£ s. d.	£ s. d.	£ s. d.
Antrim,	270 0 0	–	322 0 0	120 0 0	–	193 0 0
Belfast, Borough of,	100 0 0	–	117 0 0	116 0 0	–	81 0 0
Carrickfergus, Co. of the Town,	50 0 0	–	–	96 0 0	–	–
Clare,	334 0 0	–	128 0 0	30 0 0	–	–
Donegal,	150 0 0	158 0 0	491 0 0	223 0 0	–	10 0 0
Dublin, County of the City,	600 0 0	–	800 0 0	120 0 0	720 0	391 0 0
Galway,	270 0 0	–	222 0 0	54 0 0	–	6 0 0
Galway, County of the Town,	60 0 0	–	31 0 0	60 0 0	–	–
Kilkenny,	250 0 0	85 0 0	60 0 0	52 0 0	–	6 0 0
Kilkenny, County of the City,	30 0 0	–	10 0 0	70 0 0	–	–
Leitrim,	277 0 0	170 0 0	185 0 0	25 0 0	–	7 0 0
*Monaghan,	284 0 0	–	240 0 0	75 0 0	–	3 0 0
Tyrone,	370 0 0	50 0 0	397 0 0	111 0 0	–	40 0 0
Wexford,	107 0 0	30 0 0	47 0 0	60 0 0	–	1 0 0
Waterford, County of the City,	60 0 0	–	50 0 0	30 0 0	–	–
Totals, { [illegible]	4,384 0 0	675 0 0	3,432 0 0	1,140 0 0	720 0 0	880 0 0
Totals, { [illegible]	4,030 0 0	470 0 0	2,980 0 0	1,397 0 0	423 0 0	357 0 0
Increase,	–	–	–	–	–	–
Decrease,	350 0 0	205 0 0	470 0 0	256 0 0	297 0 0	24 0 0

* The offices of Clerk of the Crown and Clerk of the Peace in the County of Monaghan were united in

received by them, under statute, custom, or other authority, during the year 1895.

[illegible]								
On Crown [illegible] and Appeals from Magistrates' [illegible]	On Publicans' Licences [illegible]	On Civil Bill [illegible]	On [illegible]	On Registration [illegible]	[illegible] and fees not named	Total amount of [illegible]		COUNTIES, AND COUNTIES OF CITIES AND OF TOWNS, &c. (35.)
£ s. d.	£ s. d.	£ s. d.	£ s. d.	£ s. d.	£ s. d.	£ s. d.		
[illegible]	[illegible]	[illegible]	-	-	[illegible]	[illegible]		Antrim.
[illegible]	[illegible]	-	-	-	-	[illegible]		Belfast, Borough of.
-	[illegible]	-	-	-	[illegible]	[illegible]		Carrickfergus, Co. of the Town.
[illegible]	[illegible]	[illegible]	-	-	-	[illegible]		Clare.
[illegible]	[illegible]	-	-	-	-	[illegible]		Donegal.
[illegible]	[illegible]	-	[illegible]	-	-	[illegible]		Dublin, County of the City.
-	[illegible]	[illegible]	-	-	-	[illegible]		Galway.
-	[illegible]	[illegible]	-	-	-	[illegible]		Galway, County of the Town.
[illegible]	[illegible]	[illegible]	-	-	[illegible]	[illegible]		Kilkenny.
-	[illegible]	-	-	-	-	[illegible]		Kilkenny, County of the City.
-	[illegible]	[illegible]	-	-	[illegible]	[illegible]		Leitrim.
[illegible]	[illegible]	[illegible]	-	-	-	[illegible]		Monaghan.
[illegible]	[illegible]	[illegible]	-	-	[illegible]	[illegible]		Tyrone.
[illegible]	[illegible]	[illegible]	-	-	-	[illegible]		[illegible]ford.
-	[illegible]	-	-	-	-	[illegible]		Waterford, Co. of the City.
[illegible]	[illegible]	[illegible]	[illegible]	-	[illegible]	[illegible]	1895.	Total.
[illegible]	[illegible]	[illegible]	[illegible]	[illegible]	[illegible]	[illegible]	1894.	
-	-	-	-	-	-	-		Increase.
[illegible]	[illegible]	[illegible]	-	[illegible]	[illegible]	[illegible]		Decrease.

[illegible]

XIII.—SUMMARY of returns of fees and other emoluments received by Clerks of the Crown under statute, custom, or other authority, as sworn to by them at Spring and Summer Assizes of the year 1884, under Statute 6 & 7 Wm. IV., c. 116, s. 112, [illegible] salaries.

Counties, and Counties of Cities and of Towns. (a)	Salary.	[illegible] Grand Jury [illegible]	Fees paid by [illegible]	Fees other than those paid by Crown Solicitor	[illegible]	Total amount of salary, fees, [illegible]
	£ s. d.	£ s. d.	£ s. d.	£ s. d.	£ s. d.	£ s. d.
Antrim,	[illegible]	[illegible]	[illegible]	[illegible]	-	[illegible]
Carrickfergus, County of the Town,	[illegible]	-	[illegible]	[illegible]	-	[illegible]
Clare,	[illegible]	-	[illegible]	[illegible]	-	[illegible]
Donegal,	[illegible]	-	[illegible]	[illegible]	-	[illegible]
Dublin, County of the City,	-	-	[illegible]	[illegible]	-	[illegible]
Galway,	[illegible]	-	[illegible]	[illegible]	-	[illegible]
Galway, County of the Town,	[illegible]	-	[illegible]	-	-	[illegible]
Kilkenny,	[illegible]	-	[illegible]	[illegible]	-	[illegible]
Kilkenny, County of the City,	[illegible]	-	[illegible]	-	-	[illegible]
Leitrim,	[illegible]		[illegible]	[illegible]	-	[illegible]
*Monaghan,	[illegible]	-	[illegible]	-	-	[illegible]
Tyrone,	[illegible]	-	[illegible]	[illegible]	-	[illegible]
Waterford,	[illegible]	-	[illegible]	-	-	[illegible]
Waterford, County of the City,	[illegible]	-	[illegible]	-	-	[illegible]
Total, 1883,	[illegible]	[illegible]	[illegible]	[illegible]	-	[illegible]
Total, 1884,	[illegible]	[illegible]	[illegible]	[illegible]	-	[illegible]
Increase,	-	-	-	-	-	-
Decrease,	[illegible]	-	[illegible]	[illegible]	-	[illegible]

* See notes on pages [illegible] and [illegible].

XIV.—SUMMARY of Petty Sessions stamps and Crown fines, with their application.

RECEIPTS IN 1884.

	£ s. d.	£ s. d.
Petty Sessions stamps,		[illegible]
Fines,	[illegible]	
Less to parties as costs,	[illegible]	
		[illegible]
Dividends,		[illegible]
Amount transferred from Dogs Act fund,		[illegible]
		[illegible]

APPLICATION IN 1884.

	£ s. d.	£ s. d.
Officers of local courts:		
Salaries of Petty Sessions Clerks,	[illegible]	
Pensions to Petty Sessions Clerks,	[illegible]	
Salaries of Registrar and his Clerks,	[illegible]	
Expenses, &c.,	[illegible]	
		[illegible]
Police,		
Dublin Metropolitan,		—
Royal Irish Constabulary,		[illegible]
[illegible]		[illegible]
To Treasurers of boroughs,		[illegible]
Private persons,		
		[illegible]

XV.—SUMMARY of Dogs Licence Duty, and its application.

RECEIPTS IN 1884.

	£ s. d.
Dogs licence duty,	[illegible]
Dividends on moneys invested,	[illegible]
	[illegible]

APPLICATION IN 1884.

	£ s. d.
Cost of [illegible], &c.,	[illegible]
In aid of Grand Jury cess,	[illegible]
In aid of Town rates,	[illegible]
[illegible] and added to Fines and Fees Fund, by order of the Lord Lieutenant, under 44 & 45 Vic., c. 18,	[illegible]
	[illegible]

TABLE XVI.

SUMMARY of HARBOUR RECEIPTS AND EXPENDITURE.

XVI.—Summary of Dues, Tolls, Rents, and other Receipts of Harbour and Pier Authorities, for the

Name of Harbour, Dock, Pier, Quay, and Wharf.	[illegible]	Receipts.						
		Harbour, Pier, [illegible] Dues	Wharf, Pier, Quay, or Dock Dues.	[illegible] Dues.	Lighthouse or Passing Light Dues.	[illegible] Dues.	[illegible]	[illegible]
	£	£	£	£	£	£	£	£
[illegible]	-	[illegible]	-	-	-	-	-	-
[illegible]	-	-	[illegible]	-	-	-	-	[illegible]
Arklow,	[illegible]	[illegible]	-	[illegible]	-	-	-	-
[illegible]	[illegible]	[illegible]	-	-	-	-	-	-
[illegible]	[illegible]	[illegible]	-	[illegible]	-	-	-	-
[illegible]	[illegible]	[illegible]	-	-	-	-	-	-
[illegible] and [illegible],	[illegible]	[illegible]	-	-	[illegible]	-	-	-
Belfast Harbour and Docks.	[illegible]	-	[illegible]	77,491	-	-	-	-
[illegible] Pier,	[illegible]	-	-	3	-	-	-	-
Carlingford Lough,	[illegible]	[illegible]	-	-	-	-	-	-
[illegible]	[illegible]		[illegible]	[illegible]	-	-	[illegible]	-
[illegible] Castle,	[illegible]	[illegible]	-	-	-	-	-	-
Coleraine,	-	[illegible]	-	[illegible]	-	116	[illegible]	-
Cork.	[illegible]	[illegible]	-	[illegible]	-	-	-	-
[illegible]	[illegible]	[illegible]	-	[illegible]	-	-	-	-
[illegible]	[illegible]	[illegible]	-	[illegible]	[illegible]	-	-	-
[illegible]	-	-	-	-	-	-	-	[illegible]
[illegible]	[illegible]	[illegible]	-	-	-	-	-	-
Dublin,	[illegible]	[illegible]	-	-	-	[illegible]	-	-
Do. Custom House Docks.	[illegible]	-	[illegible]	-	-	-	-	-
Dundalk,	-	[illegible]	-	[illegible]	-	[illegible]	-	-
[illegible]	[illegible]	-	[illegible]	-	-	-	-	-
Dungarvan, including [illegible]	-	[illegible]	-	-	-	-	-	-
[illegible] East, Harbour, Pier, and Dock,	-	-	[illegible]	-	-	-	-	[illegible]
[illegible]	-	-	[illegible]	-	-	-	-	-
Galway,	[illegible]	[illegible]	-	-	-	[illegible]	-	-
[illegible]	-	-	[illegible]	-	-	-	-	[illegible]
[illegible] Pier,	-	[illegible]	-	-	-	-	-	-
[illegible] Quay and Harbour,	[illegible]	[illegible]	-	7	-	-	-	-
[illegible] Pier and Harbour,	[illegible]	-	[illegible]	-	-	-	-	-
Kingstown.	-	-	[illegible]	-	-	-	-	[illegible]
Kinsale.	[illegible]	[illegible]	[illegible]	[illegible]	-	-	-	-
Larne,	-	-	[illegible]	[illegible]	-	-	-	-
Limerick.	-	-	[illegible]	[illegible]	-	-	-	-
Londonderry,	-	[illegible]	[illegible]	[illegible]	[illegible]	[illegible]	-	-
[illegible] Pier,	-	-	[illegible]	-	-	-	-	-
New Ross,	[illegible]	[illegible]	[illegible]	[illegible]	-	[illegible]	-	-
[illegible]	-	-	-	-	-	-		-
[illegible]	[illegible]	[illegible]	[illegible]	[illegible]	-	-	-	-
Sligo,	[illegible]	[illegible]	-	[illegible]	[illegible]	[illegible]	-	-
Tralee and Fenit,	[illegible]	[illegible]	-	-	-	-	-	-
Waterford, including [illegible]	[illegible]	[illegible]	[illegible]	-	[illegible]	[illegible]	[illegible]	-
Westport.	[illegible]	[illegible]	[illegible]	[illegible]	-	[illegible]	-	-
Wexford.	[illegible]	[illegible]	-	[illegible]	-	[illegible]	-	-
Wicklow.	[illegible]	[illegible]	-	[illegible]	-	-	-	-
Youghal.	[illegible]	[illegible]	[illegible]	[illegible]	-	-	-	-
Total,	[illegible]	[illegible]	[illegible]	[illegible]	[illegible]	[illegible]	[illegible]	[illegible]

[illegible]

[illegible] period of twelve months for which the accounts were made up preceding 31st December, 1894.

Receipts.							
Rents, Use of Lighters, [illegible], &c.	Sale of [illegible].	Money borrowed on Security of [illegible].	Other Receipts.	Total Receipts in the year.	Balance [illegible] at the end of the year.	Total.	Name of Harbour, Dock, Pier, Quay or Wharf.
£	£	£	£	£	£	£	
-	-	-	-	[illegible]	-	[illegible]	Annalong.
6	4	-	-	[illegible]	-	[illegible]	Ardglass.
-	6	-	-	871	-	[illegible]	Arklow.
-	-	-	-	193	-	[illegible]	Balbriggan.
87	-	-	877	[illegible]	271	1,775	Ballina.
-	-	-	-	[illegible]	-	[illegible]	[illegible].
-	-	-	1	[illegible]	-	297	Baltimore and Skibbereen.
[illegible]	-	-	[illegible]	[illegible]	-	[illegible]	Belfast Harbour and Docks.
-	-	-	-	2	-	[illegible]	[illegible] Pier.
-	-	-	[illegible]	[illegible]	-	[illegible]	Carlingford Lough.
[illegible]	-	-	16	[illegible]	-	[illegible]	Carrickfergus.
-	-	-	-	[illegible]	-	[illegible]	Clare Castle.
[illegible]	-	-	[illegible]	[illegible]	[illegible]	7,[illegible]	Coleraine.
[illegible]	-	-	[illegible]	[illegible]	-	[illegible]	Cork.
[illegible]	6	[illegible]	-	[illegible]	-	[illegible]	Courtown.
-	-	-	[illegible]	[illegible]	-	[illegible]	Dingle.
[illegible]	-	-	-	[illegible]	-	[illegible]	Donaghadee.
[illegible]	5	-	[illegible]	[illegible]	-	[illegible]	Drogheda.
[illegible]	[illegible]	[illegible]	[illegible]	[illegible]	[illegible]	47,[illegible]	Dublin.
[illegible]	-	-	[illegible]	[illegible]	-	[illegible]	Do. Custom House Docks.
75	-	-	[illegible]	[illegible]	[illegible]	[illegible]	Dundalk.
-	-	-	-	[illegible]	-	7	Dunfanaghy.
1	-	-	-	[illegible]	[illegible]	[illegible]	Dungarvan, including Ballinacourty, [illegible], and Helvick.
[illegible]	-	-	-	[illegible]	-	[illegible]	Dunmore East, Harbour, Pier, and Dock.
-	-	-	-	[illegible]	[illegible]	[illegible]	Foynes.
[illegible]	-	-	-	4,[illegible]	-	[illegible]	Galway.
[illegible]	[illegible]	-	-	[illegible]	-	[illegible]	Howth.
-	-	-	-	[illegible]	[illegible]	[illegible]	[illegible] Pier.
-	-	-	-	[illegible]	-	[illegible]	[illegible] Quay and Harbour.
-	-	-	-	[illegible]	-	[illegible]	Kilrush Pier and Harbour.
[illegible]	[illegible]	-	[illegible]	[illegible]	-	[illegible]	Kingstown.
-	-	-	-	[illegible]	-	[illegible]	Kinsale.
[illegible]	-	-	[illegible]	[illegible]	-	[illegible]	Larne.
[illegible]	-	1,[illegible]	[illegible]	[illegible]	-	[illegible]	Limerick.
[illegible]	[illegible]	[illegible]	[illegible]	[illegible]	-	[illegible]	Londonderry.
-	-	-	-	[illegible]	-	16	[illegible] Pier.
-	-	-	-	[illegible]	-	[illegible]	New Ross.
-	-	-	-	-	[illegible]	[illegible]	[illegible].
-	-	-	12	[illegible]	-	[illegible]	[illegible].
[illegible]	-	[illegible]	[illegible]	[illegible]	-	[illegible]	Sligo.
-	-	-	-	[illegible]	-	[illegible]	Tralee and Fenit.
[illegible]	[illegible]	-	[illegible]	[illegible]	-	[illegible]	Waterford, including Arthurstown, Ballyhack, and Duncannon.
-	-	[illegible]	6	[illegible]	-	[illegible]	Warrenpoint.
[illegible]	-	-	[illegible]	[illegible]	-	[illegible]	Wexford.
-	-	-	12	[illegible]	-	[illegible]	Wicklow.
-	-	-	-	[illegible]	-	[illegible]	Youghal.
[illegible]	[illegible]	[illegible]	[illegible]	[illegible]	[illegible]	[illegible]	Total.

[illegible]

[illegible] VI.—continued.

XVI. (continued).—Summary of expenditure of Harbour and Pier Authorities, for the latest

[illegible]	[illegible]	[illegible]	[illegible]	[illegible]	[illegible]	[illegible]	[illegible]	[illegible]	[illegible]
	£	£	£	£	£	£	£	£	£
Ardglass,	-	[illegible]	-	-	[illegible]	-	-	-	-
[illegible]	-	[illegible]	-	-	[illegible]	-	-	-	-
Arklow,	-	[illegible]	[illegible]	-	[illegible]	-	-	-	-
Balbriggan,	-	[illegible]	[illegible]	-	[illegible]	-	-	[illegible]	-
[illegible]	-	[illegible]	[illegible]	-	[illegible]	-	[illegible]	-	[illegible]
[illegible]	-	-	-	[illegible]	-	-	-	-	-
[illegible]	-	[illegible]	[illegible]	-	-	[illegible]	[illegible]	[illegible]	[illegible]
[illegible]	-	[illegible]	-	[illegible]	[illegible]	[illegible]	-	[illegible]	[illegible]
[illegible]	-	-	-	-	[illegible]	-	-	-	-
[illegible]	-	[illegible]	[illegible]	-	[illegible]	-	[illegible]	-	[illegible]
[illegible]	-	[illegible]	[illegible]	[illegible]	77	-	-	[illegible]	[illegible]
[illegible]	-	[illegible]	[illegible]	[illegible]	[illegible]	[illegible]	-	-	-
[illegible]	[illegible]	[illegible]	[illegible]	[illegible]	[illegible]	-	[illegible]	[illegible]	-
Cork,	-	[illegible]	[illegible]	[illegible]	[illegible]	[illegible]	[illegible]	[illegible]	[illegible]
[illegible]	-	-	[illegible]	-	[illegible]	-	[illegible]	1	1
Dingle,	-	[illegible]	-	[illegible]	-	[illegible]	-	-	7
[illegible]	-	[illegible]	-	-	[illegible]	-	-	-	-
[illegible]	-	[illegible]	[illegible]	-	[illegible]	-	[illegible]	[illegible]	[illegible]
Dublin,	-	[illegible]	[illegible]	[illegible]	[illegible]	[illegible]	[illegible]	-	[illegible]
Do. [illegible]	-	[illegible]	[illegible]	[illegible]	[illegible]	-	-	-	[illegible]
Dundalk,	-	[illegible]	[illegible]	[illegible]	[illegible]	-	[illegible]	[illegible]	[illegible]
[illegible]	-	-	-	-	[illegible]	-	-	-	-
Dungarvan, including [illegible]	[illegible]	[illegible]	[illegible]	-	[illegible]	-	[illegible]	[illegible]	-
[illegible]	-	[illegible]	-	-	[illegible]	-	-	-	-
[illegible]	[illegible]	[illegible]	-	-	[illegible]	-	-	-	[illegible]
Galway,	-	[illegible]	[illegible]	-	[illegible]	-	-	[illegible]	[illegible]
Howth,	-	[illegible]	-	-	[illegible]	-	-	-	[illegible]
[illegible]	[illegible]	[illegible]	-	-	-	-	-	-	-
[illegible]	-	[illegible]	[illegible]	-	-	-	-	-	[illegible]
[illegible]	-	[illegible]	-	[illegible]	[illegible]	-	-	[illegible]	-
Kingstown,	-	[illegible]	-	10,413	[illegible]	-	-	-	-
Kinsale,	-	[illegible]	[illegible]	[illegible]	[illegible]	-	-	[illegible]	[illegible]
Larne,	-	[illegible]	1,810	-	[illegible]	-	-	[illegible]	[illegible]
Limerick,	[illegible]	[illegible]	[illegible]	-	[illegible]	-	[illegible]	[illegible]	[illegible]
Londonderry,	[illegible]	[illegible]	[illegible]	-	[illegible]	-	[illegible]	[illegible]	[illegible]
[illegible]	-	[illegible]	-	-	-	-	-	-	-
New Ross,	-	[illegible]	[illegible]	-	[illegible]	-	-	-	[illegible]
[illegible]	[illegible]	[illegible]	-	-	-	-	-	-	-
[illegible]	-	[illegible]	[illegible]	-	[illegible]	-	-	-	[illegible]
Sligo,	-	[illegible]	[illegible]	[illegible]	[illegible]	[illegible]	[illegible]	[illegible]	[illegible]
[illegible]	-	[illegible]	[illegible]	[illegible]	[illegible]	-	[illegible]	[illegible]	[illegible]
Waterford, including [illegible]	-	[illegible]	[illegible]	-	[illegible]	[illegible]	[illegible]	[illegible]	[illegible]
Westport,	-	[illegible]	[illegible]	[illegible]	[illegible]	-	-	[illegible]	[illegible]
Wexford,	-	[illegible]	[illegible]	-	[illegible]	-	[illegible]	[illegible]	[illegible]
Wicklow,	-	[illegible]	[illegible]	[illegible]	-	-	-	[illegible]	1
Youghal,	-	[illegible]	[illegible]	-	[illegible]	-	-	[illegible]	[illegible]
Total,	[illegible]	[illegible]	[illegible]	[illegible]	[illegible]	[illegible]	[illegible]	[illegible]	[illegible]

period of twelve months for which the accounts were made up preceding 31st December, 1896

Expenditure.									
[illegible]	[illegible]	Law expenses.	[illegible]	[illegible]	Other payments.	Total expenditure.	Balance in hand at the close of the year.	Total.	Name of Harbour, Dock, Pier, Quay, or Wharf.
£	£	£	£	£	£	£	£	£	
-	-	-	-	-	-	[illegible]	[illegible]	[illegible]	Annalong.
-	-	-	-	-	-	[illegible]	-	[illegible]	Ardglass.
-	-	[illegible]	-	-	[illegible]	[illegible]	[illegible]	[illegible]	Arklow.
-	-	-	-	-	-	[illegible]	[illegible]	[illegible]	Balbriggan.
[illegible]	[illegible]	[illegible]	-	-	[illegible]	[illegible]	-	[illegible]	Ballina.
-	-	-	-	-	-	[illegible]	[illegible]	[illegible]	Ballycastle.
-	-	[illegible]	-	-	[illegible]	[illegible]	[illegible]	[illegible]	Baltimore and Skibbereen.
[illegible]	[illegible]	-	-	-	[illegible]	[illegible]	[illegible]	[illegible]	Belfast Harbour and Docks.
-	-	-	-	-	-	[illegible]	[illegible]	[illegible]	Brookhaven Pier.
-	[illegible]	-	-	-	[illegible]	[illegible]	[illegible]	[illegible]	Carlingford Lough.
[illegible]	[illegible]	-	-	-	[illegible]	[illegible]	[illegible]	[illegible]	Carrickfergus.
-	-	[illegible]	-	-	[illegible]	[illegible]	[illegible]	[illegible]	Clare Castle.
[illegible]	[illegible]	-	-	-	[illegible]	[illegible]	-	[illegible]	Coleraine.
-	[illegible]	[illegible]	-	-	[illegible]	[illegible]	[illegible]	[illegible]	Cork.
-	-	-	-	-	[illegible]	[illegible]	[illegible]	[illegible]	Courtown.
-	-	-	-	-	[illegible]	[illegible]	[illegible]	[illegible]	Dingle.
-	-	-	-	-	-	[illegible]	-	[illegible]	Donaghadee.
-	[illegible]	[illegible]	-	-	[illegible]	[illegible]	[illegible]	[illegible]	Drogheda.
-	[illegible]	[illegible]	-	-	4,617	[illegible]	-	67,720	Dublin.
-	-	[illegible]	-	-	[illegible]	[illegible]	[illegible]	[illegible]	Do. Custom House Docks.
[illegible]	[illegible]	-	-	-	[illegible]	[illegible]	-	[illegible]	Dundalk.
-	-	-	-	-	-	[illegible]	[illegible]	[illegible]	Dunleary.
[illegible]	[illegible]	[illegible]	-	-	[illegible]	[illegible]	-	[illegible]	Dungarvan, including Ballinacourty, Ballinagoul, and Helvick.
-	-	-	-	-	-	[illegible]	-	[illegible]	Dunmore East, Harbour, Pier, and Dock.
[illegible]	[illegible]	-	-	-	[illegible]	[illegible]	-	[illegible]	Foynes.
[illegible]	-	-	-	-	[illegible]	[illegible]	[illegible]	[illegible]	Galway.
-	-	-	-	-	-	[illegible]	-	[illegible]	Howth.
-	-	-	-	-	-	[illegible]	-	[illegible]	Killybegs Pier.
-	[illegible]	-	-	-	[illegible]	[illegible]	[illegible]	[illegible]	Kilkee Quay and Harbour.
-	-	[illegible]	-	-	[illegible]	[illegible]	[illegible]	[illegible]	Kilrush Pier and Seafield.
-	-	-	-	-	[illegible]	[illegible]	-	[illegible]	Kingstown.
[illegible]	-	-	-	-	[illegible]	[illegible]	[illegible]	[illegible]	Kinsale.
[illegible]	[illegible]	-	-	-	-	[illegible]	[illegible]	[illegible]	Larne.
[illegible]	[illegible]	[illegible]	-	-	[illegible]	[illegible]	[illegible]	[illegible]	Limerick.
[illegible]	[illegible]	[illegible]	-	-	[illegible]	[illegible]	[illegible]	[illegible]	Londonderry.
-	-	-	-	-	1	[illegible]	[illegible]	[illegible]	Mountcharles Pier.
-	[illegible]	[illegible]	-	-	[illegible]	[illegible]	[illegible]	[illegible]	New Ross.
-	-	-	-	-	-	[illegible]	-	[illegible]	Queenstown.
-	-	-	-	-	-	[illegible]	[illegible]	[illegible]	Skerries.
[illegible]	[illegible]	[illegible]	-	-	[illegible]	[illegible]	[illegible]	[illegible]	Sligo.
[illegible]	-	[illegible]	-	-	[illegible]	[illegible]	[illegible]	[illegible]	Tralee and Fenit.
[illegible]	[illegible]	-	-	-	[illegible]	[illegible]	[illegible]	[illegible]	Waterford, including Arthurstown, Ballyhack, and Dunmore.
[illegible]	[illegible]	[illegible]	-	-	[illegible]	[illegible]	[illegible]	[illegible]	Westport.
[illegible]	[illegible]	[illegible]	-	-	[illegible]	[illegible]	[illegible]	[illegible]	Wexford.
-	-	[illegible]	-	-	[illegible]	[illegible]	[illegible]	[illegible]	Wicklow.
-	[illegible]	-	-	-	[illegible]	[illegible]	[illegible]	[illegible]	Youghal.
[illegible]	[illegible]	[illegible]	-	-	[illegible]	[illegible]	[illegible]	[illegible]	Total.

XVII.—SUMMARY of tolls and other income, with expenditure, in respect of inland Navigations

Name of Navigation.	Balance in favour at the commencement of the financial year.	Receipts. Grand Jury cess.	Tolls.	Other receipts.	Total receipts during the year.	Balance against at the close of the financial year.	Total.
	£ s. d.	£ s. d.	£ s. d.	£ s. d.	£ s. d.	£ s. d.	£ s. d.
Lough Corrib, . . .	–	[illegible]	[illegible]	–	[illegible]	–	[illegible]
Lower Bann, . . .	[illegible]	[illegible]	[illegible]	[illegible]	[illegible]	–	[illegible]
Upper Bann, . . .	–	[illegible]	[illegible]	[illegible]	[illegible]	–	[illegible]
Total, . . .	[illegible]	[illegible]	[illegible]	[illegible]	[illegible]	–	[illegible]

XVIII.—SUMMARY of tolls and other receipts, with expenditure, in respect of inland Navigations maintained [illegible] the latest period for which the accounts were made

Name of Navigation.	Balance in favour at the commencement of the financial year.	Receipts. Imperial taxes.	Grand Jury cess.	Tolls.	Other receipts.	Total receipts during the year.	Balance against at the close of the financial year.	Total.
	£ s. d.	£ s. d.	£ s. d.	£ s. d.	£ s. d.	£ s. d.	£ s. d.	£ s. d.
Lower Boyne,* . . .	–	[illegible]	–	[illegible]	–	[illegible]	–	[illegible]
Maigue (County Limerick),	–	[illegible]	–	[illegible]	–	[illegible]	–	[illegible]
Shannon, ...	–	–	–	[illegible]	[illegible]	[illegible]	[illegible]	[illegible]
Total, . .	–	[illegible]	–	[illegible]	[illegible]	[illegible]	[illegible]	[illegible]
Total of XVII. and XVIII.,	[illegible]	[illegible]	[illegible]	[illegible]	[illegible]	[illegible]	[illegible]	[illegible]

* The receipts and expenditure in connection with the Lower Boyne Navigation were for [illegible]

XIX.—SUMMARY of repayments of expenditure for Arterial drainage made to the Commissioners of Public [illegible] c. 49, during the year ended

—	Total Expenditure by Board of Works chargeable on lands and Counties.	Portion charged on County cess.	Portion charged on lands improved.	Charge not imposed.
	£ s. d.	£ s. d.	£ s. d.	£ s. d.
Under 5 & 6 Vic., c. 89, and Acts amending same, .	[illegible]	[illegible]	[illegible]	–
Under 26 & 27 Vic., c. 88, ...	*[illegible]	[illegible]	[illegible]	[illegible]
Under 26 & 27 Vic., c. 88, Maintenance works, . .	[illegible]	–	[illegible]	–
Total, ...	[illegible]	[illegible]	[illegible]	[illegible]

* This does not include [illegible]

[illegible] out of Grand Jury cess, for the year 1895, from returns by Navigation trustees.

Balance unpaid at the commencement of the financial year.	Expenditure.			Balance in ... at the close of the financial year.	Total.	Name of Navigation.
	Works.	Salaries and Incidentals.	[illegible]			
£ s. d.	£ s. d.	£ s. d.	£ s. d.	£ s. d.	£ s. d.	
[illegible]	[illegible]	[illegible]	[illegible]	–	[illegible]	Lough Corrib.
–	[illegible]	[illegible]	[illegible]	[illegible]	[illegible]	Lower Bann.
[illegible]	[illegible]	[illegible]	[illegible]	[illegible]	[illegible]	Upper Bann.
[illegible]	[illegible]	[illegible]	[illegible]	[illegible]	[illegible]	Total.

out of the Imperial taxes, or by receipts from tolls, &c., for twelve months ended the 31st of March, 1895, up previous to the 31st of December, 1895.

Balance unpaid at the commencement of the financial year.	Expenditure.			Surplus payable to the Exchequer.	Balance in favour at the close of the financial year.	Total.	Name of Navigation.
	Works.	Salaries and Incidentals.	Total.				
£ s. d.	£ s. d.	£ s. d.	£ s. d.	£ s. d.	£ s. d.	£ s. d.	
–	[illegible]	[illegible]	[illegible]	[illegible]	–	[illegible]	Lower Boyne.
–	[illegible]	[illegible]	[illegible]	[illegible]	–	[illegible]	Maigue (County Limerick)
[illegible]	[illegible]	[illegible]	[illegible]	–	–	[illegible]	Shannon.
[illegible]	[illegible]	[illegible]	[illegible]	[illegible]	–	[illegible]	Total.
[illegible]	[illegible]	[illegible]	[illegible]	[illegible]	[illegible]	[illegible]	Total of XVII. and XVIII.

of the above year only,—the Navigation having been handed over to a Company in [illegible].

Works, under 5 & 6 Vic., c. 89, and Acts amending same, and under 26 & 27 Vic., c. 88, and 29 & 30 Vic., the 31st of March, 1895.

Total expenditure during year.	Portion of expenditure made out of County cess during year.	Repayments made by proprietors of lands during year.	[illegible]
£ s. d.	£ s. d.	£ s. d.	
–	–	–	Under 5 & 6 Vic., c. 89, and Acts amending same.
[illegible]	[illegible]	[illegible]	Under 26 & 27 Vic. c. 88.
[illegible]	–	[illegible]	Under 29 & 30 Vic. c. 49, Maintenance works.
[illegible]	[illegible]	[illegible]	Total.

[illegible] were refunded, not having been expended.

XXI.—Summary of returns of fees received under the Merchant Shipping Act, 1854, during the latest period of twelve months for which the accounts were made up preceding the 31st of December, 1895.

—	Light dues.	Fees under Merchant Shipping Act, 1854. On examination of Masters and Mates.	On engagement or discharge of seamen.	On renewal of certificates.	In respect of the survey of vessels.	Totals.
	£ s. d.	£ s. d.	£ s. d.	£ s. d.	£ s. d.	£ s. d.
Commissioners of Irish Lights,	16,476 4 7	–		–	–	16,476 4 7
Ports or Place.						
Belfast,	–	110 6 0	–	8 10 10	[illegible]	1,004 17 4
Cork,	–	20 10 0	–	1 5 0	112 8 4	[illegible]
Dublin,	–	57 0 0	–	1 5 0	171 4 [illegible]	[illegible]
Galway,	–	0 7 0	–	0 17 0	[illegible]	[illegible]
Limerick,	–	–	–	[illegible]	[illegible]	[illegible]
Londonderry,	–	–	–	[illegible]	[illegible]	[illegible]
Newry,	–	–	–	[illegible]	[illegible]	[illegible]
[illegible],	–	–	–	0 0 0	[illegible]	[illegible]
Sligo,	–	–	–	–	10 0 0	10 0 0
Waterford,	–	–	–	0 10 4	[illegible]	[illegible]
Wexford,	–	–	–	–	–	–
Total,	16,476 4 7	728 17 0	–	[illegible]	5,510 17 10	[illegible]

XXII.—Balances of Loans outstanding against the several Town and Harbour Authorities,

Local Authorities.	Balances of loans from Government Loan. At Six per Cent. or upwards, or of several such Sums. At commencement of year.	At close of year.	At Five per Cent. and under Six per Cent. At commencement of year.	At close of year.	At Four per Cent. and under Five per Cent. At commencement of year.	At close of year.	Below Four per Cent. At commencement of year.	At close of year.
I. Town Councils.	£	£	£	£	£	£	£	£
Belfast,	–	–	–	–	[illegible]	[illegible]	1,1[illegible],775	[illegible]
Clonmel,	–	–	–	–	–	–	–	–
Cork,	–	–	–	–	[illegible]	[illegible]	715,[illegible]	[illegible]
Drogheda,	–	–	–	–	[illegible]	[illegible]	–	–
Dublin,	–	–	–	–	[illegible]	[illegible]	[illegible]	[illegible]
Kilkenny,	–	–	[illegible]	[illegible]	–	–	–	–
Limerick,	–	–	[illegible]	[illegible]	–	–	–	–
Londonderry,	–	–	–	–	[illegible]	[illegible]	–	–
Sligo,	–	–	–	–	14,617	[illegible]	–	–
Waterford,	[illegible]	[illegible]	–	–	–	–	[illegible]	[illegible]
Wexford,	–	–	–	–	–	–	–	–
Total,	[illegible]	[illegible]	[illegible]	[illegible]	[illegible]	[illegible]	[illegible]	[illegible]
II. Town and other Commissioners under Special Acts.								
Belfast City and District Water Commissioners.	–	–	–	–	–	–	[illegible]	[illegible]
Blackrock,	–	–	–	–	–	–	[illegible]	[illegible]
Bray,	–	–	–	–	–	–	[illegible]	[illegible]
Clontarf,	–	–	–	–	[illegible]	[illegible]	–	–
Dalkey,	–	–	[illegible]	[illegible]	–	–	–	–
Drumcondra, Clonliffe, and Glasnevin,	–	–	[illegible]	[illegible]	–	–	–	–
Kingstown,	–	–	–	–	–	–	[illegible]	[illegible]
Galway,	–	–	–	–	–	–	–	–
Kilmainham (New),	–	–	–	–	–	–	–	–
Kingstown,	–	–	–	–	[illegible]	–	–	[illegible]
Newry,	–	–	–	–	[illegible]	[illegible]	–	–
Pembroke,	–	–	–	–	–	–	[illegible]	[illegible]
Rathmines and Rathgar,	–	–	–	–	[illegible]	[illegible]	[illegible]	[illegible]
Total,	–	–	[illegible]	[illegible]	[illegible]	[illegible]	[illegible]	[illegible]
III. Commissioners under Towns Act 1854.								
Athlone,	–	–	–	–	–	–	–	–
Ballinasloe,	–	–	–	–	–	–	–	–
Ballina,	–	–	–	–	[illegible]	[illegible]	–	–
Ballymena,	–	–	–	–	–	–	–	–
Ballybay,	–	–	–	–	[illegible]	[illegible]	–	–
Ballymoney,	–	–	–	–	–	–	–	–
Ballyshannon,	–	–	–	–	–	–	–	–
Banbridge,	–	–	–	–	–	–	–	–
Bangor,	–	–	–	–	–	–	–	–
Callan,	–	–	–	–	–	–	–	–
Carlow,	–	–	–	–	–	–	–	–
Carrick-on-Suir,	–	–	–	–	–	–	–	–
Cashel,	–	–	[illegible]	[illegible]	–	–	–	–
Cavan,	–	–	–	–	–	–	–	–
Clonakilty,	–	–	–	–	–	–	–	–
Clones,	–	–	–	–	–	–	–	–
Coleraine,	–	–	–	–	[illegible]	10,[illegible]	–	–
Dunmore,	–	–	–	–	–	–	–	–
Dundalk,	–	–	1,[illegible]	1,[illegible]	–	–	–	–
*Dungarvan,	–	–	–	–	–	–	–	–

* The debts of the Sanitary Authority

XXI.—SUMMARY of returns of taxation on pawnbrokers by fees received by the City Marshal and by auctioneers of forfeited pledges in the City of Dublin, in the year 1893.

RECEIPTS.		EXPENDITURE.	
City Marshal—	£	Payments by City Marshal—	£
Paid by deputy auctioneers,	-	Police services,	-
Fees of office,	-	Incidental expenses,	-
		Balance on hand,	-
	£ -		£ -

No return received from the City Marshal for 1893.

and Joint Burial Boards, in Ireland, at close of the financial year ended in 1893.

On Annuity. At commencement of year.	On Annuity. At close of year.	At Five per Cent. At commencement of year.	At Five per Cent. At close of year.	At other rates of interest, not stated. At commencement of year.	At other rates of interest, not stated. At close of year.	Total. At commencement of year.	Total. At close of year.	Local Authorities.
£	£	£	£	£	£	£	£	I. TOWN COUNCILS.
941	-	-	-	7[illegible]	-	[illegible]	[illegible]	Belfast.
-	-	-	-	[illegible]	[illegible]	[illegible]	[illegible]	Clonmel.
-	-	-	-	[illegible]	[illegible]	[illegible]	[illegible]	Cork.
-	-	-	-	[illegible]	[illegible]	[illegible]	12,144	Drogheda.
-	-	-	-	[illegible]	[illegible]	[illegible]	[illegible]	Dublin.
-	-	-	-	[illegible]	[illegible]	[illegible]	4,946	Kilkenny.
[illegible]	[illegible]	-	-	[illegible]	[illegible]	[illegible]	[illegible]	Limerick.
[illegible]	[illegible]	-	-	[illegible]	[illegible]	[illegible]	[illegible]	Londonderry.
-	-	-	-	[illegible]	[illegible]	[illegible]	[illegible]	Sligo.
-	-	-	-	[illegible]	[illegible]	[illegible]	[illegible]	Waterford.
[illegible]	[illegible]	[illegible]	[illegible]	[illegible]	[illegible]	[illegible]	[illegible]	Wexford.
[illegible]	[illegible]	[illegible]	[illegible]	[illegible]	[illegible]	[illegible]	[illegible]	Total.
								II. TOWN AND OTHER COMMISSIONERS UNDER SPECIAL ACTS.
-	-	-	-	-	-	[illegible]	[illegible]	Belfast City and District Water Commissioners.
-	-	-	-	[illegible]	[illegible]	[illegible]	[illegible]	Blackrock.
-	-	-	-	-	-	[illegible]	[illegible]	Bray.
-	-	-	-	[illegible]	[illegible]	[illegible]	[illegible]	Clontarf.
-	-	-	-	[illegible]	[illegible]	[illegible]	[illegible]	Dalkey.
-	-	-	-	[illegible]	[illegible]	[illegible]	[illegible]	Drumcondra, Clonliffe, and Glasnevin.
-	-	-	-	[illegible]	[illegible]	[illegible]	[illegible]	[illegible]
[illegible]	[illegible]	-	-	[illegible]	[illegible]	[illegible]	[illegible]	Galway.
-	-	-	-	[illegible]	[illegible]	[illegible]	[illegible]	Kilmainham (New).
-	-	-	-	[illegible]	-	[illegible]	[illegible]	Kingstown.
-	-	-	-	-	[illegible]	[illegible]	[illegible]	Newry.
-	-	-	-	-	-	[illegible]	[illegible]	Pembroke.
[illegible]	[illegible]	-	-	-	-	[illegible]	[illegible]	Rathmines and Rathgar.
[illegible]	[illegible]	-	-	[illegible]	[illegible]	[illegible]	[illegible]	Total.
								III. TOWNS IMPROVEMENT ACT 1854.
[illegible]	[illegible]	-	-	[illegible]	[illegible]	[illegible]	[illegible]	Athlone.
-	-	[illegible]	[illegible]	-	-	[illegible]	[illegible]	Balbriggan.
-	-	-	-	-	-	[illegible]	[illegible]	Ballina.
-	-	-	-	[illegible]	[illegible]	[illegible]	[illegible]	Ballinasloe.
-	-	-	-	[illegible]	[illegible]	[illegible]	[illegible]	Ballybay.
-	-	-	-	[illegible]	[illegible]	[illegible]	[illegible]	Ballymena.
-	-	-	-	[illegible]	[illegible]	[illegible]	[illegible]	Ballymoney.
-	-	-	-	[illegible]	[illegible]	[illegible]	[illegible]	Banbridge.
-	-	-	-	[illegible]	[illegible]	[illegible]	[illegible]	Bangor.
-	-	-	-	[illegible]	[illegible]	[illegible]	[illegible]	Cahir.
-	-	-	-	[illegible]	[illegible]	[illegible]	[illegible]	Carlow.
-	-	-	-	[illegible]	[illegible]	[illegible]	[illegible]	Carrick-on-Suir.
-	-	-	-	[illegible]	[illegible]	[illegible]	[illegible]	Cashel.
-	-	-	-	[illegible]	[illegible]	[illegible]	[illegible]	Cavan.
-	-	-	-	[illegible]	[illegible]	[illegible]	[illegible]	Clonakilty.
-	-	-	-	[illegible]	[illegible]	[illegible]	[illegible]	Clones.
-	-	-	-	[illegible]	[illegible]	[illegible]	[illegible]	Coleraine.
-	-	-	-	[illegible]	[illegible]	[illegible]	[illegible]	Dromore.
-	-	-	-	[illegible]	[illegible]	[illegible]	[illegible]	Dundalk.
-	-	-	-	[illegible]	[illegible]	[illegible]	[illegible]	Dungarvan.

not included in this sum.

[R. XII.—continued.

XXII.—(continued)—BALANCES of LOANS outstanding against the several Town [illegible] year ended [illegible]

[illegible]	[illegible] At Six per Cent. [illegible]		At Five per Cent. [illegible] Six per Cent.		At Four per Cent. [illegible] Five per Cent.		Below Four per Cent.	
	At commencement of year.	At close of year.	At commencement of year.	At close of year.	At commencement of year.	At close of year.	At commencement of year.	At close of year.
III. [illegible]—continued.	£	£	£	£	£	£	£	£
Ennis,	-	-	-	-	-	-	-	-
Enniscorthy,	-	-	-	-	-	-	-	-
Fermoy,	-	-	-	-	-	-	-	-
[illegible]	-	-	-	-	-	-	-	-
Holywood,	-	-	-	-	-	-	-	-
Kilkenny,	-	-	-	-	-	-	-	-
[illegible] and [illegible],	-	-	-	-	[illegible]	[illegible]	-	-
[illegible]	-	-	-	-	-	-	-	-
Kinsale,	-	-	-	-	-	-	-	-
Letterkenny,	-	-	-	-	-	-	-	-
[illegible]	-	-	-	-	-	-	-	-
[illegible]	-	-	-	-	-	-	-	-
Lurgan,	-	-	-	-	-	-	-	-
[illegible]	-	-	-	-	-	-	-	-
Maryborough,	-	-	-	-	-	-	-	-
Mullingar,	-	-	-	-	-	-	-	-
Navan,	-	-	-	-	-	-	-	-
[illegible]	-	-	-	-	-	-	-	-
New Ross,	-	-	-	-	-	-	-	-
Newtownards,	-	-	[illegible]	[illegible]	-	-	-	-
[illegible]	-	-	-	-	-	-	-	-
Portadown,	-	-	-	-	-	-	[illegible]	[illegible]
Queenstown,	-	-	4,120	[illegible]	-	-	-	-
[illegible]	-	-	-	-	-	-	-	-
Strabane,	-	-	-	-	1,727	[illegible]	-	-
Templemore,	-	-	-	-	-	-	-	-
Thurles,	-	-	-	-	-	-	-	-
[illegible]	-	-	[illegible]	[illegible]	-	-	-	-
[illegible]	-	-	-	-	-	-	-	-
[illegible]	-	-	-	-	-	-	-	-
Warrenpoint,	-	-	-	-	-	-	-	-
Total,	-	-	[illegible]	[illegible]	[illegible]	[illegible]	[illegible]	[illegible]
IV. [illegible]								
Armagh,	-	-	-	-	-	-	-	-
[illegible]	-	-	[illegible]	[illegible]	-	-	-	-
[illegible]	-	-	-	-	[illegible]	[illegible]	-	-
*Youghal,	-	-	[illegible]	[illegible]	-	-	-	-
Total,	-	-	[illegible]	[illegible]	[illegible]	[illegible]	-	-
V. [illegible]								
[illegible]	-	-	-	-	-	-	-	-
[illegible]	-	-	-	-	-	-	-	-
[illegible]	-	-	-	-	-	-	-	-
[illegible]	-	-	-	-	-	-	-	-
[illegible]	-	-	-	-	-	-	-	-
[illegible]	-	-	-	-	[illegible]	[illegible]	[illegible]	[illegible]
[illegible]	-	-	-	-	-	-	-	-
[illegible]	-	-	-	-	-	-	-	-
[illegible]	-	-	-	-	-	-	-	-
[illegible]	-	-	[illegible]	[illegible]	[illegible]	[illegible]	-	-
Cork,	-	-	-	-	[illegible]	[illegible]	-	-
[illegible]	-	-	-	-	-	-	-	-
[illegible]	-	-	-	-	[illegible]	[illegible]	-	-
Dublin,	-	-	-	-	[illegible]	[illegible]	[illegible]	[illegible]
Dundalk,	-	-	-	-	[illegible]	[illegible]	-	-
[illegible]	-	-	-	-	-	-	-	-
Galway,	-	-	-	-	[illegible]	[illegible]	-	-
[illegible]	[illegible]	[illegible]	-	-	-	-	-	-
[illegible]	-	-	-	-	-	-	-	-
[illegible]	-	-	-	-	-	-	-	-
[illegible]	-	-	-	-	-	-	-	-
Limerick,	-	-	-	-	-	-	-	-
Londonderry,	-	-	-	-	-	-	[illegible]	[illegible]
New Ross,	-	-	[illegible]	[illegible]	-	-	-	-
Sligo,	-	-	-	-	[illegible]	[illegible]	-	-
[illegible]	-	-	-	-	-	-	-	-
Waterford,	-	-	-	-	-	-	-	-
[illegible]	-	-	-	-	-	-	-	-
Wexford,	-	-	-	-	[illegible]	[illegible]	-	-
Wicklow,	-	-	-	-	[illegible]	[illegible]	-	-
Total,	[illegible]	[illegible]	[illegible]	[illegible]	[illegible]	[illegible]	[illegible]	[illegible]
VI. [illegible]								
[illegible]	-	-	-	-	-	-	-	-
[illegible]	-	-	-	-	-	-	-	-
[illegible]	-	-	-	-	-	-	-	-
Youghal,	-	-	-	-	-	-	-	-
Total,	-	-	-	-	-	-	-	-

* The [illegible] of the [illegible] authority [illegible] in this case. [illegible]

and Harbour Authorities, and joint Burial Boards, in Ireland, at close of the financial in 1886

Sanitary loans. On Annuity. At commencement of year.	At close of year.	At Five per Cent. At commencement of year.	At close of year.	At other rate of interest, not stated. At commencement of year.	At close of year.	Total. At commencement of year.	At close of year.	Local Authorities.
£	£	£	£	£	£	£	£	III. Commissioners under Act 1854—continued.
-	-	-	-	11,879	11,897	11,879	11,897	Kells.
-	-	-	-	2,442	2,897	2,442	[illegible]	Letterkenny.
-	-	-	-	12,824	12,781	12,824	12,781	Fermoy.
-	-	-	-	63	828	63	828	Granard.
-	-	-	-	8,241	8,116	8,241	8,116	Holywood.
-	-	-	-	[illegible]	[illegible]	[illegible]	[illegible]	[illegible]
-	-	-	-	[illegible]	[illegible]	[illegible]	[illegible]	Killiney and Ballybrack.
-	-	-	-	[illegible]	[illegible]	1,175	[illegible]	[illegible]
-	-	-	-	[illegible]	[illegible]	[illegible]	[illegible]	[illegible]
[illegible]	[illegible]	-	-	-	-	[illegible]	[illegible]	[illegible]
[illegible]	[illegible]	-	-	[illegible]	[illegible]	[illegible]	17,478	Lismore.
-	-	-	-	[illegible]	[illegible]	[illegible]	[illegible]	Listowel.
[illegible]	[illegible]	-	-	[illegible]	[illegible]	[illegible]	[illegible]	Lurgan.
-	-	-	-	[illegible]	116	[illegible]	116	[illegible]
-	-	-	-	[illegible]	[illegible]	[illegible]	[illegible]	Maryborough.
-	-	-	-	[illegible]	[illegible]	[illegible]	[illegible]	Monaghan.
-	-	-	-	3,617	[illegible]	[illegible]	[illegible]	Navan.
-	-	-	-	[illegible]	[illegible]	[illegible]	1,631	Nenagh.
-	-	-	-	[illegible]	[illegible]	[illegible]	[illegible]	New Ross.
-	-	-	-	[illegible]	[illegible]	[illegible]	[illegible]	Newtownards.
-	-	-	-	[illegible]	[illegible]	[illegible]	[illegible]	Parsonstown.
-	-	-	-	[illegible]	[illegible]	[illegible]	[illegible]	Portadown.
[illegible]	[illegible]	[illegible]	[illegible]	[illegible]	[illegible]	[illegible]	[illegible]	Queenstown.
-	-	-	-	[illegible]	[illegible]	[illegible]	[illegible]	[illegible]
-	-	-	-	-	-	[illegible]	[illegible]	[illegible]
-	-	-	-	[illegible]	[illegible]	[illegible]	[illegible]	Tipperary.
-	-	-	-	[illegible]	[illegible]	[illegible]	[illegible]	Thurles.
[illegible]	[illegible]	-	-	[illegible]	[illegible]	[illegible]	[illegible]	Tralee.
-	-	-	-	[illegible]	[illegible]	[illegible]	[illegible]	[illegible]
-	-	-	-	[illegible]	[illegible]	[illegible]	[illegible]	Tuam.
-	-	-	-	[illegible]	[illegible]	[illegible]	[illegible]	Warrenpoint.
[illegible]	[illegible]	[illegible]	[illegible]	[illegible]	[illegible]	[illegible]	[illegible]	Total.
								IV. Commissioners under Act 1828.
-	-	-	-	[illegible]	[illegible]	[illegible]	[illegible]	Armagh.
-	-	-	-	-	-	[illegible]	[illegible]	[illegible]
-	-	-	-	[illegible]	[illegible]	[illegible]	[illegible]	Wicklow.
[illegible]	[illegible]	-	-	[illegible]	[illegible]	[illegible]	[illegible]	Youghal.
[illegible]	[illegible]	-	-	[illegible]	[illegible]	[illegible]	[illegible]	Total.
								V. Harbour Authorities.
-	-	-	-	[illegible]	[illegible]	[illegible]	[illegible]	[illegible]
[illegible]	[illegible]	-	-	-	-	[illegible]	[illegible]	[illegible]
[illegible]	[illegible]	-	-	-	-	[illegible]	[illegible]	Arklow.
[illegible]	[illegible]	-	-	-	-	[illegible]	[illegible]	[illegible]
-	-	-	-	[illegible]	[illegible]	[illegible]	[illegible]	Ballina.
-	-	-	-	[illegible]	[illegible]	[illegible]	[illegible]	Belfast.
-	-	-	-	[illegible]	[illegible]	[illegible]	[illegible]	Carlingford Lough.
-	-	-	-	[illegible]	[illegible]	[illegible]	[illegible]	Carrickfergus.
-	-	-	-	[illegible]	[illegible]	[illegible]	[illegible]	[illegible]
[illegible]	[illegible]	-	-	-	-	[illegible]	[illegible]	Coleraine.
-	-	-	-	-	-	[illegible]	[illegible]	Cork.
-	-	-	-	[illegible]	[illegible]	[illegible]	[illegible]	[illegible]
-	-	-	-	-	-	[illegible]	[illegible]	Drogheda.
-	-	-	-	-	-	[illegible]	[illegible]	Dublin.
-	-	-	-	[illegible]	[illegible]	[illegible]	[illegible]	Dundalk.
-	-	-	-	[illegible]	[illegible]	[illegible]	[illegible]	[illegible]
[illegible]	[illegible]	-	-	-	-	[illegible]	[illegible]	Galway.
-	-	-	-	-	-	[illegible]	[illegible]	Killala.
-	-	-	-	[illegible]	[illegible]	[illegible]	[illegible]	[illegible]
-	-	[illegible]	[illegible]	-	-	[illegible]	[illegible]	[illegible]
-	-	-	-	[illegible]	[illegible]	[illegible]	[illegible]	Larne.
[illegible]	[illegible]	-	-	[illegible]	[illegible]	[illegible]	[illegible]	Limerick.
-	-	-	-	-	-	[illegible]	[illegible]	Londonderry.
-	-	-	-	-	-	[illegible]	[illegible]	New Ross.
-	-	-	-	[illegible]	-	[illegible]	[illegible]	Sligo.
[illegible]	[illegible]	-	-	-	-	[illegible]	[illegible]	Tralee.
-	-	-	-	[illegible]	[illegible]	[illegible]	[illegible]	Waterford.
-	-	-	-	[illegible]	[illegible]	[illegible]	[illegible]	Westport.
-	-	-	-	-	-	[illegible]	[illegible]	Wexford.
[illegible]	[illegible]	-	-	-	-	[illegible]	[illegible]	Wicklow.
[illegible]	[illegible]	[illegible]	[illegible]	[illegible]	[illegible]	[illegible]	[illegible]	Total.
								VI. Joint Burial and Urban Sanitary Boards.
-	-	-	-	[illegible]	[illegible]	[illegible]	[illegible]	Banbridge.
-	-	-	-	[illegible]	[illegible]	[illegible]	[illegible]	Dundalk.
-	-	-	-	[illegible]	[illegible]	[illegible]	[illegible]	Newtownards.
-	-	-	-	[illegible]	[illegible]	[illegible]	[illegible]	Youghal.
-	-	-	-	[illegible]	[illegible]	[illegible]	[illegible]	Total.

[illegible] of the Town Authority are included in this case.

XXIII.—Table showing the towns in Ireland which are Urban Sanitary Districts; the [illegible] for the financial year ended in 18[illegible], the sums received under the Probate Duties (Scotland and Ireland) Act in respect of the year ended the 31st of March, 18[illegible], by each of those [illegible] entitled to share in the grant provided by that Act; the population and valuation of each District; the area in acres; and the Acts under which these towns are constituted.

Total number of urban sanitary districts, ... 7[illegible]

Urban Sanitary Districts.	[illegible]	[illegible]	Population.	Valuation in 18[illegible].	Area in Acres.	Acts under which constituted.
1.	2.	3.	4.	5.	6.	7.
Armagh, . . .	[illegible]	[illegible]	[illegible]	[illegible]	[illegible]	[illegible]
[illegible]	[illegible]	[illegible]	[illegible]	[illegible]	[illegible]	[illegible]
Total for [illegible] towns,		[illegible]				

[illegible]

XXIV.—TABLE showing the towns in Ireland which are not Urban Sanitary Districts; the rates made for the financial year ended in 1876; the population and valuation of each town; its area in acres; and the Act under which it is constituted.

Total number of such towns, ... 46.

NAME. 1	[illegible] 2	Population. 3	Valuation in [illegible]. 4	Area in Acres. 5	Act under which constituted. 6
	s. d.		£		
[illegible]	[illegible]	[illegible]	[illegible]	[illegible]	17 and 18 Vic., cap. 103.
[illegible]	[illegible]	[illegible]	[illegible]	[illegible]	do.
[illegible]	[illegible]	[illegible]	[illegible]	[illegible]	do.
[illegible]	[illegible]	[illegible]	[illegible]	[illegible]	do.
[illegible]	[illegible]	[illegible]	[illegible]	[illegible]	do.
[illegible]	[illegible]	[illegible]	[illegible]	[illegible]	do.
[illegible]	[illegible]	[illegible]	[illegible]	[illegible]	do.
[illegible]	[illegible]	[illegible]	[illegible]	[illegible]	do.
[illegible]	[illegible]	[illegible]	[illegible]	[illegible]	do.
[illegible]	[illegible]	[illegible]	[illegible]	[illegible]	do.
[illegible]	[illegible]	[illegible]	[illegible]	[illegible]	[illegible] Geo. IV., cap. [illegible]
*Bantry,	—	[illegible]	[illegible]	[illegible]	17 and 18 Vic., cap. 103.
[illegible]	[illegible]	[illegible]	[illegible]	[illegible]	do.
Callan,	—	[illegible]	[illegible]	[illegible]	do.
[illegible]	[illegible]	[illegible]	[illegible]	[illegible]	do.
[illegible]	[illegible]	[illegible]	[illegible]	[illegible]	do.
[illegible]	[illegible]	[illegible]	[illegible]	[illegible]	do.
[illegible]	[illegible]	[illegible]	[illegible]	[illegible]	do.
[illegible]	[illegible]	[illegible]	[illegible]	[illegible]	do.
[illegible]	[illegible]	[illegible]	[illegible]	[illegible]	do.
[illegible]	[illegible]	[illegible]	[illegible]	[illegible]	[illegible] Geo. IV., cap. [illegible]
[illegible]	—	[illegible]	[illegible]	[illegible]	do.
[illegible]	[illegible]	[illegible]	[illegible]	[illegible]	17 and 18 Vic., cap. 103.
[illegible]	[illegible]	[illegible]	[illegible]	[illegible]	do.
[illegible]	[illegible]	[illegible]	[illegible]	[illegible]	do.
[illegible]	[illegible]	[illegible]	[illegible]	[illegible]	do.
[illegible]	[illegible]	[illegible]	[illegible]	[illegible]	do.
[illegible]	[illegible]	[illegible]	[illegible]	[illegible]	do.
[illegible]	[illegible]	[illegible]	[illegible]	[illegible]	do.
[illegible]	[illegible]	[illegible]	[illegible]	[illegible]	do.
[illegible]	[illegible]	[illegible]	[illegible]	[illegible]	do.
[illegible]	[illegible]	[illegible]	[illegible]	[illegible]	do.
[illegible]	[illegible]	[illegible]	[illegible]	[illegible]	do.
[illegible]	[illegible]	[illegible]	[illegible]	[illegible]	do.
[illegible]	[illegible]	[illegible]	[illegible]	[illegible]	do.
[illegible]	[illegible]	[illegible]	[illegible]	[illegible]	do.
[illegible]	[illegible]	[illegible]	[illegible]	[illegible]	[illegible] Geo. IV., cap. [illegible]
[illegible]	[illegible]	[illegible]	[illegible]	[illegible]	17 and 18 Vic., cap. 103.
[illegible]	[illegible]	[illegible]	[illegible]	[illegible]	do.
[illegible]	[illegible]	[illegible]	[illegible]	[illegible]	do.
[illegible]	[illegible]	[illegible]	[illegible]	[illegible]	do.
[illegible]	[illegible]	[illegible]	[illegible]	[illegible]	do.
Tipperary,	[illegible]	[illegible]	[illegible]	[illegible]	do.
[illegible]	—	[illegible]	[illegible]	[illegible]	do.
[illegible]	[illegible]	[illegible]	[illegible]	[illegible]	do.
Westport,	[illegible]	[illegible]	[illegible]	[illegible]	do.

* The provisions of the Towns Improvement Act, [illegible], were adopted in Bantry in the month of July, [illegible], as already mentioned.

Table XXV.—VALUATION OF COUNTIES.

[illegible]	[illegible]	[illegible]	[illegible]	[illegible]	[illegible]
	£	£	£	£	£
Antrim,	[illegible]	[illegible]	[illegible]	[illegible]	[illegible]
Armagh,	[illegible]	[illegible]	[illegible]	[illegible]	[illegible]
Carlow,	[illegible]	[illegible]	[illegible]	[illegible]	[illegible]
Carrickfergus, County of the Town,	[illegible]	[illegible]	[illegible]	[illegible]	[illegible]
Cavan,	[illegible]	[illegible]	[illegible]	[illegible]	[illegible]
Clare,	[illegible]	[illegible]	[illegible]	[illegible]	[illegible]
Cork,	[illegible]	[illegible]	[illegible]	[illegible]	[illegible]
Cork, County of the City,	[illegible]	[illegible]	[illegible]	[illegible]	[illegible]
Donegal,	[illegible]	[illegible]	[illegible]	[illegible]	[illegible]
Down,	[illegible]	[illegible]	[illegible]	[illegible]	[illegible]
Drogheda, County of the Town,	[illegible]	[illegible]	[illegible]	[illegible]	[illegible]
Dublin,	[illegible]	[illegible]	[illegible]	[illegible]	[illegible]
Dublin, County of the City,	[illegible]	[illegible]	[illegible]	[illegible]	[illegible]
Fermanagh,	[illegible]	[illegible]	[illegible]	[illegible]	[illegible]
Galway,	[illegible]	[illegible]	[illegible]	[illegible]	[illegible]
Galway, County of the Town,	[illegible]	[illegible]	[illegible]	[illegible]	[illegible]
Kerry,	[illegible]	[illegible]	[illegible]	[illegible]	[illegible]
Kildare,	[illegible]	[illegible]	[illegible]	[illegible]	[illegible]
Kilkenny,	[illegible]	[illegible]	[illegible]	[illegible]	[illegible]
Kilkenny, County of the City,	[illegible]	[illegible]	[illegible]	[illegible]	[illegible]
King's County,	[illegible]	[illegible]	[illegible]	[illegible]	[illegible]
Leitrim,	[illegible]	[illegible]	[illegible]	[illegible]	[illegible]
Limerick,	[illegible]	[illegible]	[illegible]	[illegible]	[illegible]
Limerick, County of the City,	[illegible]	[illegible]	[illegible]	[illegible]	[illegible]
Londonderry,	[illegible]	[illegible]	[illegible]	[illegible]	[illegible]
Longford,	[illegible]	[illegible]	[illegible]	[illegible]	[illegible]
Louth,	[illegible]	[illegible]	[illegible]	[illegible]	[illegible]
Mayo,	[illegible]	[illegible]	[illegible]	[illegible]	[illegible]
Meath,	[illegible]	[illegible]	[illegible]	[illegible]	[illegible]
Monaghan,	[illegible]	[illegible]	[illegible]	[illegible]	[illegible]
Queen's County,	[illegible]	[illegible]	[illegible]	[illegible]	[illegible]
Roscommon,	[illegible]	[illegible]	[illegible]	[illegible]	[illegible]
Sligo,	[illegible]	[illegible]	[illegible]	[illegible]	[illegible]
Tipperary, North Riding,	[illegible]	[illegible]	[illegible]	[illegible]	[illegible]
Tipperary, South Riding,	[illegible]	[illegible]	[illegible]	[illegible]	[illegible]
Tyrone,	[illegible]	[illegible]	[illegible]	[illegible]	[illegible]
Waterford,	[illegible]	[illegible]	[illegible]	[illegible]	[illegible]
Waterford, County of the City,	[illegible]	[illegible]	[illegible]	[illegible]	[illegible]
Westmeath,	[illegible]	[illegible]	[illegible]	[illegible]	[illegible]
Wexford,	[illegible]	[illegible]	[illegible]	[illegible]	[illegible]
Wicklow,	[illegible]	[illegible]	[illegible]	[illegible]	[illegible]
Total,	[illegible]	[illegible]	[illegible]	[illegible]	[illegible]

XVI.—Return showing the towns of which the [illegible] the [illegible] within the [illegible] under their jurisdiction, with the County charges contributed to by them, &c.

[illegible]

[illegible]

[illegible]	[illegible]	[illegible]		[illegible]	[illegible]
		[illegible]	[illegible]		
1	2	3	4	5	6
[illegible]					
[illegible]	[illegible]	[illegible]	[illegible]	[illegible]	[illegible]
[illegible]	Do.	[illegible]	[illegible]		[illegible]
[illegible]	Do.	[illegible]	[illegible]	[illegible]	[illegible]
[illegible]	Do.	[illegible]	[illegible]	[illegible]	[illegible]
[illegible]	Do.	—	[illegible]	[illegible]	[illegible]
[illegible]	Do.	[illegible]	[illegible]	[illegible]	[illegible]
[illegible]	Do.	[illegible]	[illegible]	[illegible]	[illegible]

[illegible]

[illegible]	[illegible]	[illegible]		[illegible]	[illegible]
		[illegible]	[illegible]		
[illegible]	[illegible]	[illegible]	[illegible]	[illegible]	[illegible]
[illegible]	[illegible]	—	[illegible]	[illegible]	[illegible]
[illegible]	[illegible]	—	[illegible]	[illegible]	[illegible]
[illegible]	[illegible]	[illegible]	[illegible]	[illegible]	[illegible]
[illegible]	[illegible]	[illegible]	[illegible]	[illegible]	[illegible]
[illegible]	[illegible]	[illegible]	[illegible]	[illegible]	[illegible]
[illegible]	[illegible]	[illegible]	[illegible]	[illegible]	[illegible]
[illegible]	[illegible]	[illegible]	[illegible]	[illegible]	[illegible]

DUBLIN CASTLE,

12th *December*, 1896.

SIR,

I have to acknowledge the receipt of your letter of the 10th instant, forwarding, for submission to His Excellency the Lord Lieutenant, the Returns of Local Taxation in Ireland during the Year 1895.

I am, Sir,

Your obedient servant,

J. B. DOUGHERTY.

The Secretary,

Local Government Board,

Custom House.

www.ingramcontent.com/pod-product-compliance
Lightning Source LLC
Chambersburg PA
CBHW021537270326
41930CB00008B/1296
* 9 7 8 3 7 4 2 8 0 1 2 7 2 *